The Voice of
ENLIGHTENED
MONKS
THE THERAGATHA

One of the books of the Pali Canon
Found in the Khuddaka Nikāya

A translation into English from the Sinhala translation
by Venerable Kiribathgoda Gnānānanda Thera

A Mahamegha Publication

The Voice of Enlightened Monks: the Theragātha
by Venerable Kiribathgoda Gnānānanda Thera

Published April 2015

Computer Typesetting by

Mahamevnawa Buddhist Monastery, Toronto
Markham, Ontario, Canada L6C 1P2
Telephone: 905-927-7117

www.mahamevnawa.ca

Published by

Mahamegha Publishers
Waduwawa, Yatigaloluwa, Polgahawela, Sri Lanka.
Telephone: +94 37 2053300 | 77 3216685
www.mahameghapublishers.com
mahameghapublishers@gmail.com

Contents

Section of Single Verses

Section of Two Verses

Section of Three Verses

Section of Six Verses

Section of Seven Verses

Section of Eight Verses

Section of Nine Verses

Section of Eleven Verses

Section of Twelve Verses

Section of Thirteen Verses

Section of Fourteen Verses

Section of Sixteen Verses

Section of Twenty Verses

Introduction

The Arahant

It is sweet even to hear the sound of the word "Arahant." To be able to meet a venerable Arahant is an extremely fortunate event. In this human world, living among the humans, walking on this earth, these Arahants belong to a group of marvelous humans.

Arahants Cannot Be Measured

In this universe, these magnificent beings only appear with the help of a fully enlightened Buddha. This is because it is only under the instruction of the Buddha that the Noble Eight-Fold Path which leads to the attainment of the fruit of Stream-entry, Once-returning, Non-returning, and Arahantship is revealed. Therefore it is impossible to measure these Arahants who have achieved the ultimate purity, having destroyed all defilements.

> "Monk Upasīva, there is no way to measure an Arahant who has achieved extinguishing, Nibbāna. If someone uses an ordinary unit of measurement to measure ordinary people, Arahants cannot be measured in this way. Once all defilements have been eradicated, all arguments cease."

> *Upasīva Sutta, Sutta Nipāta verse 1076*

Like Golden Swans

For an ordinary person, it is impossible to comprehend the life of Arahants. An Arahant's life is unimaginably peaceful, simple, and liberated. In this world the only person that walks with perfect freedom is an Arahant. In this time period the very first person to become an Arahant was the fully enlightened Buddha. The Buddha spoke about the lives of Arahants in this way:

> "Arahants are well established in the Four Establishments of Mindfulness. They are not bound by craving. Like the swans that fly away from the lake, they let go of everything, large and small."
>
> *Dhammapada, verse 91*

The Tamed Arahant

If the six sense bases are completely tamed in someone, that person is definitely an Arahant. The tameness that arises from virtue, concentration, and wisdom is mind-blowing. This is the exact reason that they are extremely humble.

> "An Arahant tames his senses with the same skill that an expert horse tamer tames his horses. Because of this they become utterly extinguished. Humble and with unshakeable minds, these unblemished Arahants are a pleasant sight, even for the gods."
>
> *Dhammapada, verse 94*

Beautiful Is the Place They Reside

The Arahant sages who do wholesome actions, who speak wholesome words, and who think wholesome thoughts, make even the environment around them become beautiful. The liberated personality of these Arahant monks matches the beauty of nature very well. Like the beauty of a flower, they possess an untarnished, inherent beauty.

"Whether it be a village, a jungle, a valley, a hill or any other place, if Arahants dwell there, that place is truly delightful."

Dhammapada, verse 98

Glowing with Wisdom

Possessing an enchanting wisdom, our Great Teacher, the Buddha, shared his knowledge with his disciples. Those disciples used the power of the Buddha's enchanting wisdom to stimulate their own wisdom. It was because of that power of wisdom that they were able to rise above the ordinary people. The Buddha explained that point in this way:

"A beautiful, fragrant lotus blooms in a mud-hole filled with filth along the highway road. In the same way, in the world with its ignorant, worldly people that have stained and impure beliefs, a disciple of the Buddha will stand out among them, shining with brilliant wisdom."

Dhammapada, verses 58 & 59

The Realization of an Arahant

One becomes an Arahant by realizing the Four Noble Truths fully. That realization must occur in three phases and twelve modes. The Blessed One explained this fact in his very first discourse—the Dhammacakkappavattana Sutta.

When one becomes a stream enterer, that disciple attains the first phase with regard to the Four Noble Truths. It is known as "the knowledge of the truth."

The Knowledge of the Truth

The one who attained the Knowledge of the Truth embraces the first factor of the Noble Eight-fold Path. This means he has within himself the right view that comes from the understanding of the Four Noble Truths. He knows by his own understanding: suffering as a noble truth, the cause of suffering as a noble truth, the end of suffering as a noble truth, and that the path that must be followed to end suffering is the Noble Eight-fold Path as a noble truth. This is the Knowledge of the Truth.

The Knowledge of the Task to Be Accomplished

This is the second phase. In the first phase, the disciple understood the knowledge of the truth with regards to the Four Noble Truths. In this second phase, the disciple should have the knowledge of the task to be accomplished with regard to each noble truth. He understands that the noble truth of suffering is to be fully understood, the noble truth of the cause of suffering is to be abandoned, the noble truth of the end of suffering is to be realized, and the way leading to the end of suffering is to be developed in terms of virtue, concentration, and wisdom. This way the disciple of the Buddha realizes the Four Noble Truths completely, having established on the knowledge of the Four Noble Truths itself.

The Knowledge That the Task Has Been Completed

In this way, when one has started to develop the Noble Eightfold Path, he is capable of developing the thirty-seven aids to enlightenment. Within it, the three-fold way of training called virtue, concentration, and wisdom is developed. Then, he becomes liberated from all defilements and becomes enlightened. Having completed the task with regard to the Four Noble Truths he possesses the Knowledge That the Task Has Been Completed.

This means he has the knowledge that what had to be done with regard to the Noble Truth of Suffering has been completed. That is, the complete understanding of the Noble Truth of Suffering. He has the knowledge that what had to be done with regard to the Noble Truth of the Cause of Suffering has been completed. That is, the complete eradication of the Noble truth of the Cause of Suffering. He has the knowledge that what had to be done with regard to the Noble Truth of the End of Suffering has been completed. That is, the achievement of the Noble Truth of the End of Suffering. He has the knowledge that what had to be done with regard to the Noble Truth of the way leading to the End of Suffering has been completed in terms of virtue, concentration, and wisdom. That is, the development of the Noble Truth of the way leading to the End of Suffering. This is the third phase.

In this way, we have passed through an era where thousands of Arahants lived with the all-encompassing knowledge of the Four Noble Truths.

Inspired Utterances of Arahants

There are accounts mentioned in the Dhamma that those Arahants uttered inspired utterances about this amazing transformation which took place in their lives:

"Birth is destroyed. The holy life has been lived. What had to be done to attain enlightenment has been done. There is nothing more to be done to attain enlightenment."

The Era of a Buddha

The era of a Buddha occurs extremely rarely in the world. During that time, the chance to be born human and to come across the teaching of the Buddha is known as a time of momentous fortune. This moment in a human life is an extremely rare occurrence. Arahants are the only ones that make maximum use of this fruitful moment.

Each discourse of the Buddha contains teachings that solely lead to Arahantship in this very life. There aren't any other hidden meanings within it. Wise people are skillful in understanding that fact. With that knowledge, they place confidence in the Buddha. Furthermore, they strongly believe in the ultimate solution presented by the Buddha. They give the highest priority to realizing it. They abandon the home life and go forth into homelessness and become monks.

The Buddha's Path

The Buddha's path is a name given for the way leading to Nibbāna, preached by the Buddha.

Sabba pāpassa akaraṇaṁ
Kusalassa upasampadā
Sacitta pariyodapanaṁ
Etaṁ Buddhāna sāsanaṁ

"To abstain from all evil, to cultivate the thirty-seven aids to enlightenment, and to cleanse your own mind, this is the teaching of all Buddhas."

Dhammapada, verse 183

Entering the Buddha's Path

Entering the Buddha's path means that you embrace the Three Refuges and receive the full ordination. After that, one is gradually tamed, all the way up to Arahantship. It is because of this that Arahants utter the inspired utterance saying "Kataṁ buddhassa sāsanaṁ" (the Buddha's path has been fully followed).

The Buddha had this unsurpassed, extraordinary ability to guide the disciples who enter the path until Arahantship is reached. There is an occasion in the Middle Length Discourses where the Buddha explains the instructions on taming his disciples to a brāhmin named Gaṇaka Moggallāna in the Gaṇaka Moggallāna Sutta (Majjhima Nikāya 107).

Instructions from the Buddha

"Just as, brāhmin, when a clever horse-trainer obtains a fine thoroughbred horse, he first makes him get used to wearing the bit, and afterwards trains him further, so too when a person comes to the Tathāgata to be tamed, he first disciplines him thus: 'Come monk, be virtuous, restrained with the restraint of the major code of discipline, possess courteous behavior and good conduct, and seeing fear in the slightest fault, train in the precepts you have undertaken.'

Guard Your Sense Faculties

"When, brāhmin, the monk is virtuous... and seeing fear in the slightest fault, trains in the precepts he has undertaken, then the Tathāgata disciplines him further: 'Come, monk, guard the doors of your sense faculties. On seeing a form with the eye, do not grasp at its signs and features. Since, if you were to leave the eye faculty unguarded, evil unwholesome states of desire and anger might invade you, therefore practice the way of its restraint, guard the eye faculty, undertake the restraint of the eye faculty. On hearing a sound with the ear... On smelling an odour with the nose... On tasting a flavour with the tongue... On touching a tangible with the body... On cognizing a mind-object with the mind, do not grasp at its signs and features. Since, if you were to leave the mind faculty unguarded, evil unwholesome states of desire and anger might invade you, therefore practice the way of its restraint, guard the mind faculty, and practice the restraint of the mind faculty.'

Take Meals with Full Awareness

"When, brāhmin, the monk guards the doors of his sense faculties, then the Tathāgata disciplines him further: 'Come, monk, be moderate in eating. Reflecting wisely, you should take food, neither for fun nor for intoxication nor for the sake of physical beauty and attractiveness, but only for the endurance and continuance of this body, for ending painful feelings, and for assisting the holy life, considering: "Thus I shall give up old feelings without making new feelings and I shall be healthy and blameless and shall live in comfort.'

Meditating with Wakefulness

"When, brāhmin, the monk is moderate in eating, then the Tathāgata disciplines him further: 'Come, monk, be devoted to meditation with wakefulness. During the day, while walking back and forth and sitting, clean your mind of states that block it. In the first part of the night, while walking back and forth and sitting, clean your mind of states that block it. In the middle part of the night you should lie down on the right side in the lion's pose with one foot overlapping the other, mindful and fully aware, after noting in your mind the time for wakening up. After rising in the morning, in the third part of the night, while walking back and forth and sitting, clean your mind of states that block it.'

Be Mindful of Your Body Position and Daily Routines

"When, brāhmin, the monk is devoted to wakefulness, then the Tathāgata disciplines him further: 'Come, monk, be possessed of mindfulness and full attentiveness. Act in full awareness when going forward and returning; act in full awareness when looking ahead and looking away; act in full awareness when flexing and stretching your limbs; act in full awareness when wearing your robes and carrying your double robe and bowl; act in full awareness when eating, drinking, consuming food, and tasting; act in full awareness when defecating and urinating; act in full awareness when walking, standing, sitting, falling asleep, waking up, talking, and keeping silent.' (This means that one should not allow unwholesome states to arise)

Live in Seclusion

"When, brāhmin, the monk possesses mindfulness and full awareness, then the Tathāgata disciplines him further: 'Come, monk, spend time in a secluded resting place: the forest, the root of a tree, a mountain, a ravine, a hillside cave, a charnel ground, a jungle thicket, an open space or a heap of straw.'

Give Up the Five Hindrances

"He resorts to a secluded resting place: the forest... a heap of straw. On returning from his alms round, after his meal he sits down, folding his legs crosswise, setting his body straight, and establishing mindfulness on the meditation object. Giving up greed for the world, he lives with a mind free from greed; he purifies his mind from greed. Giving up ill will and hatred, he lives with a mind free from ill will, compassionate for the wellbeing of all living beings; he cleans his mind of ill will and hatred. Giving up sleepiness and drowsiness, he lives free from sleepiness and drowsiness, able to perceive light, mindful and fully aware; he purifies his mind from sleepiness and drowsiness. Giving up restlessness and remorse, he lives without an agitated mind and is peaceful inside; he purifies his mind from restlessness and remorse. Giving up doubt, he lives having gone beyond doubt, without confusion about wholesome states; he purifies his mind from doubt.

He Attains Jhānas

"Having thus given up these five hindrances, imperfections of the mind that weaken wisdom, quite secluded from sensual pleasures, secluded from unwholesome states, he enters upon and stays in the first jhāna, which has by applied and sustained thought, with rapture and pleasure born of seclusion.

"With the stilling of applied and sustained thought, he enters upon and stays in the second jhāna, which has self-confidence and singleness of mind without applied and sustained thought, with rapture and pleasure born of concentration.

"With the fading away as well of rapture, he lives in equanimity, and mindful and fully aware, still feeling pleasure with the body, he enters upon and stays in the third jhāna, because of which noble ones announce: 'He has a pleasant abiding who has equanimity and is mindful.'

"With the abandoning of pleasure and pain, and with the previous disappearance of joy and grief, he enters upon and stays in the fourth jhāna, which has neither-pain-nor-pleasure and purity of mindfulness due to equanimity.

"This is my instruction, brāhmin, to those monks who are in the higher training, whose minds have not yet attained the goal of Arahantship, who live hoping to achieve the supreme security from bondage.

"But these things lead to both to a pleasant living here and now and to mindfulness and full awareness for those monks who are arahants with taints destroyed, who have lived the holy life, done what had to be done, laid down the burden of defilements, reached the goal gradually, destroyed the things that tie one to existence, and are completely liberated through final knowledge."

In this manner, having developed the knowledge of seeing things as they really are, that monk contemplates all formations as impermanent, suffering, and non-self. Through the realization of the Four Noble Truths, he becomes liberated from suffering.

Marvelous Lives

Now you have learned about the incredible gradual training used by the Buddha to discipline his disciples. The Buddha explained about the noble lives of his enlightened disciples who were fully tamed under that instruction in this way:

> "Monks, to whatever extent there are dwelling places of beings, even up to the peak of existence, Arahants are the foremost in the world, Arahants are the Supreme.

> *Paṭama Arahanta Sutta, SN 22.76*

Verses of Enlightened Monks

Through this sacred book, you will meet the noble sages who attained enlightenment when the Buddha was alive.

These exalted sages achieved the essence of the Buddha's path: the liberation through Arahantship and final extinguishing. The account of their struggle for enlightenment is amazing. It is hard to imagine how they practiced the Dhamma with such extreme energy, and determination, even at a risk to their own lives.

Saying "Saṅghaṁ saraṇaṁ gacchāmi," we go for refuge to this community of noble disciples. How exalted and pure they are! We who are living in the twenty-sixth century of the Buddhist era can be overjoyed simply by recollecting the pure lives of such enlightened disciples.

While you are reading this sacred book, those Arahants might seem to appear in front of you. You will feel like they are conversing with you. You will witness before you the display of the ultimate purity of their hearts. The community of the Buddha's noble disciples is absolutely remarkable and magnificent.

Venerable resident monks in the Mahamewnawa Meditation Monastery, members of the Maha Sangha, and faithful devotees supported me in compiling this sacred book. May they achieve the Supreme bliss of Nibbāna!

May our noble friends, Mr. Dayawamsa Jayakodi and Mrs. Jayakodi, and their staff who aided in of the publishing of this sacred book, also achieve Nibbāna! May you who read this book attain Nibbāna in this Gautama Buddha's path!

Ven. Kiribathgoda Ñāṇānanda Thero

Mahamewnāwa Meditation Monastery
Vaduwāwa, Yatigaloluwa
Polgahawela
Telephone: 037-2244602

Recollecting the Exalted Qualities of the Community of Noble Monks

Supaṭipanno Bhagavato Sāvaka Saṅgho

The community of noble disciples of the Buddha is dedicated to the path of the eradication of passion, hatred and delusion by the three-fold training of virtue, concentration, and wisdom. Of pure conduct is the community of disciples, of the Blessed One—Supatipanno. I go for refuge and pay homage to the community of disciples!

Ujupaṭipanno Bhagavato Sāvaka Saṅgho

The community of the noble disciples of the Buddha is dedicated to following the straight way called the Noble Eightfold Path. Of upright conduct is the community of disciples of the Blessed One—Ujupaṭipanno. I go for refuge and pay homage to the community of disciples!

Ñāyapaṭipanno Bhagavato Sāvaka Saṅgho

The community of noble disciples of the Buddha is dedicated to the realization of the Four Noble Truths. Of wise conduct is the community of disciples of the Blessed One—Ñāyapaṭipanno. I go for refuge and pay homage to the community of disciples!

Sāmīcipaṭipanno Bhagavato Sāvaka Saṅgho

The community of the noble disciples of the Buddha is dedicated to propagating the pure teachings of the Supremely Enlightened Buddha with utmost respect. Of generous conduct is the community of disciples of the Blessed One—Sāmīcipaṭipanno. I go for refuge and pay homage to the community of disciples!

Yadidam cattāri purisayugāni aṭṭha purisapuggalā esa Bhagavato sāvakasaṅgho

The community of the noble disciples of the Blessed One consists of four pairs of persons:

1. The disciple practicing the path for the attainment of Stream-entry and the Stream-entrant.
2. The disciple practicing the path for the attainment of Once-returning and the Once-returner.
3. The disciple practicing the path for the attainment of Non-returning and the Non-returner.
4. The disciple practicing the path for the attainment of Arahantship and the Arahant.

The community of the noble disciples of the Blessed One consists of the eight kinds of individuals:

1. The disciple practicing the path for the attainment of Stream-entry.
2. The Stream-entrant.
3. The disciple practicing the path for the attainment of Once-returning
4. The Once-returner.
5. The disciple practicing the path for the attainment of Non-returning
6. The Non-returner.
7. The disciple practicing the path for the attainment of Arahantship
8. The Arahant.

I go for refuge and pay homage to the community of disciples of the Blessed One!

Āhuneyyo Bhagavato sāvakasaṅgho

The community of noble disciples of the Buddha is worthy of offerings that are brought from far away, such as robes, alms food, resting places and medicine. I go for refuge and pay homage to the community of disciples of the Blessed One!

Pāhuneyyo Bhagavato sāvakasaṅgho

The community of noble disciples of the Buddha is worthy of hospitality. I go for refuge and pay homage to the community of disciples of the Blessed One!

Dhakkineyyo Bhagavato sāvakasaṅgho

The community of noble disciples of the Buddha is worthy of gifts that are offered by the donors expecting great fruits and results. I go for refuge and pay homage to the community of disciples of the Blessed One!

Añjalikaranīyo Bhagavato sāvakasaṅgho

The community of noble disciples of the Buddha is worthy of reverential salutations by humans and gods. I go for refuge and pay homage to the community of disciples of the Blessed One!

Anuttaraṁ Puññakkhettaṁ lokassā ti

The community of noble disciples of the Buddha is the incomparable field of merit that aids beings to accumulate merit. I go for refuge and pay homage to the community of disciples of the Blessed One!

Sadhu! Sadhu! Sadhu!

*Homage to the Blessed One, the Worthy One,
the Supremely Enlightened One!*

Verses of Introduction
Nidāna Gāthā

The Liberated Ones developed their minds through this excellent Dhamma. Listen carefully to the verses uttered by them about their lives. Indeed, these verses are like the roar of cave dwelling lions with strong teeth.

These Enlightened Ones are known by various names and clans. They are endowed with various attainments. They have liberated from all suffering.

They attained extinguishing, Nibbāna, through deep penetration by insight. Truly, reflecting on the perfect Dhamma taught by their superb master, the Buddha, these enlightened ones uttered these sweet verses.

Section of Single Verses

The Verse of Arahant Subhūti

1. I stay in a roofed hut; it is very comfortable. The wind does not disturb me. Dear rain cloud, rain as much as you want. My mind has become perfectly still and is liberated from all defilements. I live with great energy. Dear rain cloud, rain as much as you want.

This verse was said by Arahant Subhūti.

The Verse of Arahant Mahākoṭṭhita

2. This monk's senses are very calm. He has restrained himself from all evil. He speaks with full awareness. He is not proud. Just as the wind shakes off a leaf of a tree, this monk has shaken off all unwholesome things.

This verse was said by Arahant Mahākoṭṭhita.

The Verse of Arahant Kaṅkhārevata

3. There is a person who can remove the doubt of the people who go to him. He is the Buddha. See the excellent wisdom of the Buddhas! It is like a fire blazing at midnight. That wisdom gives beings bright knowledge and the eye of the Dhamma.

This verse was said by Arahant Kaṅkhārevata.

The Verse of Arahant Puṇṇa

4. One should only associate with wise, superior people who show the way to goodness. Their understanding is extremely subtle. They practice the Dhamma heedfully. These wise, superior people have realized the deepest meaning of life - the Four Noble Truths that are profound, subtle and hard to understand.

This verse was said by Arahant Puṇṇa.

The Verse of Arahant Dabba

5. Superior tamer of people, the great Supreme Buddha tamed someone who was difficult to tame. Now this person lives with extraordinary happiness. He is freed from doubt. He won the battle over defilements. This monk, Dabba, who has no fear at all, will attain final extinguishing at passing away, having established his mind in Nibbāna.

This verse was said by Arahant Dabba.

The Verse of Arahant Sītavaniya

6. This monk lives in the Sīta forest. He lives alone and spends his time very happily. He has become perfectly still. He won the battle over defilements. Being freed from hair standing on end, this wise monk protects his mindfulness regarding the body.

This verse was said by Arahant Sītavaniya.

The Verse of Arahant Bhalliya

7. Just as a great flood pushes away a log bridge, this monk pushed away the armies of Māra. He won the battle over defilements. He doesn't have any fear at all. He is tamed in the Dhamma. Having established his mind in Nibbāna, this monk will attain final extinguishing at passing away.

This verse was said by Arahant Bhalliya.

The Verse of Arahant Vīra

8. Superior tamer of people, the great Supreme Buddha tamed someone who was difficult to tame. Now this person lives with extra ordinary happiness. He is freed from doubt. He won the battle over defilements. Having established his mind in Nibbāna this monk "Vīra" who has no hair standing on end at all will attain final extinguishing at passing away.

This verse was said by Arahant Vīra.

The Verse of Arahant Pilindavaccha

9. My arrival into the Buddha's path has truly benefited me. Coming to him never hurt me. This opinion of mine is not wrong. The excellent Nibbāna, which is well expounded in the Dhamma, is the Nibbāna I have attained.

This verse was said by Arahant Pilindavaccha.

The Verse of Arahant Puṇṇamāsa

10. This monk understood the Dhamma to the maximum level. He is calm and has a tamed mind. He abandoned all desires for himself and for other people. He doesn't have any attachments to anything at all. Now he understands very well how the world arises and passes away.

This verse was said by Arahant Puṇṇamāsa.

The Verse of Arahant Cūlavaccha

11. This monk is overjoyed with the Dhamma taught by the Buddha. He was able to attain excellent Nibbāna where all formations such as merit and demerit are appeased.

This verse was said by Arahant Cūlavaccha.

The Verse of Arahant Mahāvaccha

12. He is very strong in wisdom. He is virtuous and mindful. He always likes to be in Jhāna (meditations) with a still mind. He eats knowing the purpose of eating. This desireless monk is awaiting time to attain final extinguishing at passing away.

This verse was said by Arahant Mahāvaccha.

The Verse of Arahant Vanavaccha

13. In the forest where I live, pure streams of cool water are blue like the sky. The surrounding area is also very beautiful. The

mountains are lit up by fireflies at night. I delight in these mountains.

This verse was said by Arahant Vanavaccha.

The Verse of Arahant Vanavaccha's Pupil

14. My preceptor said to me, "Sīvaka, let's leave this village and head to the forest." (I'm having the same idea.) Even though my body lives in the village, my mind is in the forest. Even though I sleep in the village, my mind goes to the forest. There is no attachment for someone who understands the true reality of this life.

This verse was said by Arahant Vanavaccha's pupil.

The Verse of Arahant Kuṇḍadhāna

15. One should cut off five [fetters that bind beings to the sensual realm.] One should abandon five [fetters that bind beings to form and formless realms.] One should especially develop the five [faculties of confidence, energy, mindfulness, concentration and wisdom.] The monk who has gone beyond the five [ties of lust, hatred, delusion, conceit and views] is called a "flood-crosser."

This verse was said by Arahant Kuṇḍadhāna.

The Verse of Arahant Bellaṭṭhisīsa

16. There was a great bull with beautiful horns. Even when the bull was tied to the ploughshare, it went at ease. In this same way, the days and nights pass by very easily for me. I experience this kind of ease because I have attained spiritual happiness.

This verse was said by Arahant Bellaṭṭhisīsa.

The Verse of Arahant Dāsaka

17. The foolish and sleepy one eats too much food because of his greediness. Then he sleeps rolling to all sides. His life is like that

of a pig that is full from eating filth. This fool will come to the womb again and again.

This verse was said by Arahant Dāsaka.

The Verse of Arahant Siṅgālapitu

18. The monk who lives in the Bhesakala forest is an heir of the Buddha's Dhamma. Having meditated on the skeletal body, he could cover up the whole earth with that object. I think he will get rid of sensual lust very quickly.

This verse was said by Arahnt Siṅgālapitu.

The Verse of Arahant Kuṇḍala

19. Irrigators can lead water to wherever they need. Arrow makers can bend the arrows as they wish. Carpenters can bend wood as they wish. In this same way, superior people can tame themselves as they wish.

This verse was said by Arahant Kuṇḍala.

The Verse of Arahant Ajita

20. I'm not scared of death nor do I have a desire to live. Mindfully and with clear awareness, I will abandon my body.

This verse was said by Arahant Ajita.

The Verse of Arahant Nigrodha

21. I'm not scared of suffering in this round of rebirth. Our great teacher is well skilled in showing the way to Nibbāna. By following the Noble Eightfold Path, monks reach Nibbāna where there is no fear of suffering in saṁsāra.

This verse was said by Arahant Nigrodha.

The Verse of Arahant Cittaka

22. The peacocks that live in the Kāranci forest have beautiful blue necks. As a chorus they sing beautiful songs. Maybe peacocks like the cool breeze, and that is why their voices are so sweet. Their sweet voice can awaken those who are sleeping and make those who are meditating happy.

This verse was said by Arahant Cittaka.

The Verse of Arahant Gosāla

23. I accepted the great Buddha's advice with much respect. That day I ate milk rice with honey. Then I sat under the shade of a bunch of bamboo trees and started meditating. I contemplated how suffering arises and ceases based on the five aggregates of clinging. Living in seclusion is key for me, therefore I will go back to the Sānu forest again.

This verse was said by Arahant Gosāla.

The Verse of Arahant Sugandha

24. It's been only a year since I have become a monk. See the excellence of this Dhamma! I too achieved the Triple Knowledge. The Buddha's path has been fully followed by me.

This verse was said by Arahant Sugandha.

The Verse of Arahant Nandiya

25. This monk has attained the great fruit of Arhantship and lives with a mind that is lit with wisdom. Hey Māra! Are you going to fall into suffering for bothering this kind of monk?

This verse was said by Arahant Nandiya.

The Verse of Arahant Ubhaya

26. I heard the Dhamma well taught by the Supreme Buddha, the one born into the clan of the sun. I too could realize the very

subtle Four Noble Truths, just as an archer pierces the tip of a hair with his arrow.

This verse was said by Arahant Ubhaya.

The Verse of Arahant Lomasakaṅgiya

27. I don't need any grasses such as dabba, kusa, potakila, usira, munja, and bulrushes. I will throw them out. My only intent is seclusion.

This verse was said by Arahant Lomasakaṅgiya.

The Verse of Arahant Jambugāmikaputta

28. You don't waste time looking for cloths to make robes, do you? You don't want to decorate your body, do you? The fragrance of your virtue spreads all around, doesn't it? Such a fragrance doesn't spread from other people.

This verse was said by Arahant Jambugāmikaputta.

The Verse of Arahant Hārita

29. Hārita, free your mind from laziness. Straighten your mind, just as an arrow maker straightens out his arrow. Then, split ignorance.

This verse was said by Arahant Hārita.

The Verse of Arahant Uttiya

30. As soon as I got sick, I came to my senses: "Now I am sick. Time has come for me to practice the Dhamma diligently without being lazy."

This verse was said by Arahant Uttiya.

The Verse of Arahant Gabbharatīriya

31. This monk lives in the middle of the thick forest. When mosquitos and flies attack him, he endures mindfully, just like a king elephant in battle.

This verse was said by Arahant Gabbharatīriya.

The Verse of Arahant Suppiya

32. I shall escape from this aging life and shall head to unaging Nibbāna. I shall escape from this stressful life and shall head to peaceful Nibbāna. I shall head to that unsurpassed Nibbāna, the greatest freedom.

This verse was said by Arahant Suppiya.

The Verse of Arahant Sopāka

33. Just as a mother is caring towards her only child, one should care for all beings.

This verse was said by Arahant Sopāka.

The Verse of Arahant Posiya

34. A well learned monk always thinks it's very important to stay away from women. One day I came from the forest and went home, but I got up from the bed and left without taking leave from anyone. My name is Posiya.

This verse was said by Arahant Posiya.

The Verse of Arahant Sāmaññakāni

35. He practices the Noble Eightfold Path. That is the only straight way leading to Nibbāna. When one practices path factors, wishing for happiness, one will gain happiness. His good reputation spreads and his fame grows.

This verse was said by Arahant Sāmaññakāni.

The Verse of Arahant Kumāputta

36. Listening to the Dhamma is excellent. Living according to the Dhamma is even more excellent. Living without craving is always excellent. Investigating the meaning of the Dhamma is also very excellent. Accepting the Dhamma respectfully is excellent. Practicing these things is called "living the true monk life without defilements."

This verses was said by Arahant Kumāputta.

The Verse of Arahant Kumāputta's Friend

37. Unrestrained people waste their time walking all around through cities and countries. They will never achieve one-pointedness of mind. What is the purpose of roaming all over? Stop doing things to get revenge. Don't give in to craving; meditate instead.

This verse was said by Arahant Kumāputta's Friend.

The Verse of Arahant Gavampati

38. He could stop the Sarabhu River from flowing using his supernormal powers. This monk, Gavampati, is freed from defilements and craving. This great sage overcame all ties and has crossed over existence. Even gods come to worship this great sage.

This verse was said by Arahant Gavampati.

The Verse of Arahant Tissa

39. Just as someone looks for help immediately after being hit by a sword, and just as someone immediately tries to put out a fire on his head, with strong mindfulness a monk should immediately try to eradicate sensual desire.

This verse was said by Arahant Tissa.

The Verse of Arahant Vaḍḍhamāna

40. Just as someone looks for help immediately after being hit by a sword, and just as someone immediately tries to put out a fire on his head, with strong mindfulness a monk should immediately try to eradicate desire for existence.

This verse was said by Arahant Vaḍḍhamāna.

The Verse of Arahant Sirivaḍḍha

41. Flashes of lightning fall upon the flat land between the Vebhāra and Pāṇḍava mountains. A monk meditates in a cave between these mountains. He can't be compared to a statue. This monk is a son of the Buddha who has an unagitated mind.

This verse was said by Arahant Sirivaḍḍha.

The Verse of Arahant Khadiravaniya

42. Dear novices Cāla, Upacāla, Sisupacāla, are you well established in mindfulness? Look! Just now, your uncle Sāriputta Bhante came here. That Bhante is much, much smarter than an extremely skilled archer.

This verse was said by Arahant Khadiravaniya.

The Verse of Arahant Sumaṅgala

43. It is good that I am freed! It is good that I am freed! it is good that I am freed from three crooked things. I am freed from the sickles. I am freed from the ploughs. I am freed from the curved spades. Even though they are here, I don't need any of them. Yes, I do not need any of them. Dear Sumaṅgala, now meditate. Yes, dear Sumaṅgala, now meditate. Dear Sumaṅgala, practice the Dhamma diligently without being lazy.

This verse was said by Arhant Sumaṅgala.

The Verse of Arahant Sānu

44. Mother! People cry when someone dies or when they don't see their loved ones who are alive. But, mother, why do you cry for me when I am alive and seen?

This verse was said by Arahant Sānu.

The Verse of Arahant Ramaṇīyavihāri

45. Just as the great bull trips and is right about to fall, but catches itself and prevents falling, so too I became an insightful disciple of the fully enlightened Buddha.

This verse was said by Arahant Ramaṇīyavihāri.

The Verse of Arahant Samiddhi

46. Having given up my house, I became a monk truly out of faith. Mindfulness and wisdom are well developed in me. My mind has also become perfectly still. [Hey Māra,] do all kinds of nasty things to me, but I will not be disturbed.

This verse was said by Arahant Samiddhi.

The Verse of Arahant Ujjaya

47. Great hero, the Supreme Buddha, I pay homage to you. You live freed from all suffering. Following your great example, I too became liberated from the taints.

This verse was said by Arahant Ujjaya.

The Verse of Arahant Sañjaya

48. Since I became a monk, having given up my house, I don't recall having any ignoble, angry thoughts.

This verse was said by Arahant Sañjaya.

The Verse of Arahant Rāmaṇeyyaka

49. In the midst of the loud noise of these birds and squirrels, there is no agitation in my mind. It is because my mind delights only in Nibbāna.

This verse was said by Arahant Rāmaṇeyyaka.

The Verse of Arahant Vimala

50. The earth is sprinkled, the cold wind blows, lightning flashes in the distant sky. Distracting thoughts in my mind are also fading away. My mind is becoming perfectly still.

This verse was said by Arahant Vimala.

The Verse of Arahant Godhika

51. The rain falls like a sweet song. My small roofed hut is very comfortable. The window is closed. My mind is becoming perfectly still. Therefore rain cloud, rain as much as you please.

This verse was said by Arahant Godhika.

The Verse of Arahant Subāhu

52. The rain falls like a sweet song. My small roofed hut is very comfortable. The window is closed. My mind is becoming perfectly still on mindfulness of the body. Therefore rain cloud, rain as much as you please.

This verse was said by Arahant Subāhu.

The Verse of Arahant Valliya

53. The rain falls like a sweet song. My small roofed hut is very comfortable. The window is closed. Staying in this hut, I practise Dhamma diligently without being lazy. Therefore rain cloud, rain as much as you please.

This verse was said by Arahant Valliya.

The Verse of Arahant Uttiya

54. The rain falls like a sweet song. My small roofed hut is very comfortable. The window is closed. I stay in this hut, freed from craving. Therefore rain cloud, rain as much as you please.

This verse was said by Arahant Uttiya.

The Verse of Arahant Añjanavaniya

55. From the day I came to the Añjana Forest, I used this reclining chair as my hut. I achieved the Triple Knowledge. The Buddha's path has been fully followed by me.

This verse was said by Arahant Añjanavaniya.

The Verse of Arahant Kuṭivihāri

56. Who is in that small hut? There is a desireless monk with a perfectly still mind in this hut. Therefore friend, know this: the making of this little hut for you was not in vain.

This verse was said by Arahant Kuṭivihāri.

The Verse of Arahant Dutiya Kuṭivihāri

57. This hut is very old. Do you desire a new hut? Give up that desire for a new hut. Dear monk, a new hut means just another suffering.

This verse was said by Arahant Dutiya Kuṭivihāri.

The Verse of Arahant Ramaṇiya Kuṭivihāri

58. My hut is very beautiful and delightful. This was made for me out of faith. But I don't need girls. Go, women. Go to people who need you.

This verse was said by Arahant Ramaṇiya Kuṭivihāri.

The Verse of Arahant Kosalavihāri

59. I became a monk out of faith. A small hut was also made for me in the forest. I live in that hut practicing the Dhamma diligently, energetically, wisely and mindfully.

This verse was said by Arahant Kosalavihāri.

The Verse of Arahant Sīvali

60. I came to live in this hut having a high intention in my mind. I have accomplished my intention. I achieved realization of the Noble Truths and liberation from suffering. I uprooted conceit completely from my mind.

This verse was said by Arahant Sīvali.

The Verse of Arahant Vappa

61. Only the one with eye of Dhamma sees the reality of life. He recognizes the superior person and the inferior person. But the one who doesn't see the reality of life doesn't recognize the superior person or the inferior person.

This verse was said by Arahant Vappa.

The Verse of Arahant Vajjiputta

62. We live alone in the forest like thrown away logs. But many people like our lives very much. They look at us wishfully, like hell beings looking at those who go to heaven.

This verse was said by Arahant Vajjiputta.

The Verse of Arahant Pakkha

63. I saw an eagle that was holding a piece of meat. It slipped from his mouth and dropped from the sky to the ground. Other eagles swarmed and fought over the piece of meat. I did all that was

required to attain Nibbāna. I only desired Nibbāna, therefore I achieved supreme happiness through happiness.

This verse was said by Arahant Pakkha.

The Verse of Arahant Vimalakoṇḍañña

64. He was born to Ambapāli [the famous courtesan] and the very famous King Bimbisāra. Holding up the flag of wisdom he stomped on the flag of conceit along with the huge flag of Māra.

This verse was said by Arahant Vimalakoṇḍañña.

The Verse of Arahant Ukkhepakatavaccha

65. The monk Ukkhepakatavaccha retained this Dhamma in his mind for many years. Established on this very Dhamma, he preaches it to the lay disciples with a delightful heart.

This verse was said by Arahant Ukkepakatavaccha.

The Verse of Arahant Meghiya

66. The great hero, the Supreme Buddha who realized everything about the world, advised me. I took that great advice into my heart. Having established mindfulness in me I then lived with the Supreme Buddha. I too achieved the Triple Knowledge. The Buddha's path has been fully followed by me.

This verse was said by Arahant Meghiya.

The Verse of Arahant Ekadhammasavanīya

67. I burned out all the defilements in my mind. I uprooted all existence. Journeying on from rebirth to rebirth has completely ended. There is no more rebirth for me.

This verse was said by Arahant Ekadhammasavanīya.

The Verse of Arahant Ekudāniya

68. Whoever developed the mind, practiced the Dhamma diligently and trained in the Noble Path of sages has an unagitated mind. He has a peaceful life. That sage who always lives with clear mindfulness doesn't have anything that creates suffering.

This verse was said by Arahant Ekudāniya.

The Verse of Arahant Channa

69. This Dhamma preached with the excellent wisdom of the Supreme Buddha has an amazing taste and an extraordinary value. Having heard that Dhamma, I entered the path to Nibbāna. My only intention was to attain Nibbāna. Our great teacher, the Supreme Buddha, shows this path with an incredible ability.

This verse was said by Arahant Channa.

The Verse of Arahant Puṇṇa

70. Virtue is a great thing in this Dhamma path. But the greatest thing is developed wisdom. Through one's virtue and wisdom, one can achieve victory among humans and gods.

This verse was said by Arahant Puṇṇa.

The Verse of Arahant Vacchapāla

71. One should always associate with noble people who are wise, humble, full of good qualities, and have realized the Noble Truths with a very subtle and skilled understanding. It's not difficult for someone to attain Nibbāna if one associates with such noble people.

This verse was said by Arahant Vacchapāla.

The Verse of Arahant Ātuma

72. Just as a young bamboo tree with its branches and foliage is hard to cut away from the clump, so too I find it very hard to

get permission from my wife to become a monk. I am the one who brought my wife to my house. But I became a monk. Please, mother, approve this.

This verse was said by Arahant Ātuma.

The Verse of Arahant Māṇava

73. Having seen an old man, a miserable sick person, and a dead person come to the end of his life, I gave up delightful sensual pleasures and, having given up the home life, I became a monk.

This verse was said by Arahant Māṇava.

The Verse of Arahant Suyāma

74. He has no sense desire, no anger, no drowsiness and sleepiness, no restlessness and remorse, no doubt at all.

This verse was said by Arahant Suyāma.

The Verse of Arahant Susārada

75. How wonderful is the sight of great noble people whose minds are well established in the Dhamma! As a result of that association, one's doubt is removed and wisdom is developed. That association can even make a fool become wise. Therefore association with superior people is always great.

This verse was said by Arahant Susārada.

The Verse of Arahant Piyañjaha

76. In the presence of noble people full of good virtues and wisdom he is ready to kneel down. In the presence of the people who lack good virtues and wisdom, he is ready to stand up. Among incelibate (sexually active) people, he is celibate. Among the people who seek delight in sensual pleasures, he lives detached from sensual pleasures.

This verse was said by Arahant Piyañjaha.

The Verse of Arahant Hatthārohaputta

77. Previously, my mind wandered where it wished, where it liked, as it pleased. But now, having warned the mind with developed wisdom I have control over it as a hook-holder controls a vicious elephant.

This verse was said by Arahant Hatthārohaputta.

The Verse of Arahant Meṇḍasira

78. I have run through the journeying-on of numerous rebirths, since I didn't have the knowledge to stop this cycle of suffering. Even though I was born with suffering, now I have put an end to all suffering.

This verse was said by Arahant Meṇḍasira.

The Verse of Arahant Rakkhita

79. I have eliminated all desire, all hatred has been rooted out, and all delusion is gone. I have become cool and extinguished.

This verse was said by Arahant Rakkhita.

The Verse of Arahant Ugga

80. Whatever kamma was done by me, whether small or great, all that is completely destroyed. There is no more rebirth for me.

This verse was said by Arahant Ugga.

The Verse of Arahant Samatigutta

81. Whatever evil was done by me previously in other births, that I have to experience only in this life. I won't have any other lives.

This verse was said by Arahant Samatigutta.

The Verse of Arahant Kassapa

82. Dear son, while journeying, go to places that are safe, have no fear, and offer good alms. Do not fall into trouble by going to strange places.

This verse was said by Arahant Kassapa.

The Verse of Arahant Sīha

83. Dear Sīha, remain diligent practicing the Dhamma, not relaxing day or night. Develop wholesome qualities. Eradicate defilements as soon as possible.

This verse was said by Arahant Sīha.

The Verse of Arahant Nīta

84. Sleeping all night, delighting in company by day, when indeed will the fool put an end to the suffering of saṁsāra?

This verse was said by Arahant Nīta.

The Verse of Arahant Sunāga

85. He is well skilled at developing a meditation object for the one-pointedness of mind. He knows the sweetness of solitude very well. He meditates well. He is prudent and mindful. He gains spiritual happiness.

This verse was said by Arahant Sunāga.

The Verse of Arahant Nāgita

86. Apart from the Buddha's path, a person from a different religion doesn't have a path like this leading to Nibbāna. Pointing out this fact, Our Blessed One instructs the monks as though he is showing something on his palm.

This verse was said by Arahant Nāgita.

The Verse of Arahant Paviṭṭha

87. The true nature of this suffering of the five aggregates of clinging has been understood by me. All existences have been split. Journeying on from rebirth to rebirth has completely ended. Now there is no more rebirth for me.

This verse was said by Arahant Paviṭṭha.

The Verse of Arahant Ajjuna

88. Once my life was swept away in the flood of saṁsāra, just as a person is swept away by a great flood. As a result of comprehending the Four Noble Truths, I was finally able to get away from the flood and step on dry land.

This verse was said by Arahant Ajjuna.

The Verse of Arahant Devasabha

89. These sensual pleasures are like a pile of mud. Yes, really like a pile of mud. I crossed over all sensual pleasures. Feelings are like a cliff. I avoided all those feelings. I escaped from the great flood of saṁsāra and the ties of defilements. All conceits are destroyed.

This verse was said by Arahant Devasabha.

The Verse of Arahant Sāmidatta

90. I understood the suffering of the five aggregates of clinging completely. Now just the aggregates with the uprooted roots remain. Journeying on from rebirth to rebirth is completely ended. There is no more rebirth for me.

This verse was said by Arahant Sāmidatta.

The Verse of Arahant Paripuṇṇaka

91. Today I enjoy the taste of Supreme Nibbāna. Such a taste cannot be found in any food in this human world. Even the heav-

enly food called Shudha doesn't have such taste. Gotama Buddha taught this excellent Dhamma with an unlimited realization.

This verse was said by Arahant Paripuṇṇaka.

The Verse of Arahant Vijaya

92. All the taints in his life were destroyed. Now he doesn't have any desire, even for food. His mind now is only focused on the meditation objects of emptiness, signlessness, and non-establishment. That monk's Dhamma path is impossible to find, just as the paths of birds are impossible to find in the air.

This verse was said by Arahant Vijaya.

The Verse of Arahant Eraka

93. Dear Eraka, sensual pleasures are very painful. Dear Eraka, sensual pleasures are not happy. Dear Eraka, he who desires sensual pleasures desires pain. Dear Eraka, he who doesn't desire sensual pleasures, doesn't desire pain.

This verse was said by Arahant Eraka.

The Verse of Arahant Mettaji

94. Homage to the Blessed One, the Supreme Buddha, Great Son of the Sakaya clan. The Supreme Buddha, possessor of the foremost qualities, taught us a foremost Dhamma.

This verse was said by Arahant Mettaji.

The Verse of Arahant Cakkhupāla.

95. Since my eyes were destroyed, I became blind. I have entered this wilderness road. If I am too weak to move forward, I will sleep right here in this spot. But I will never go with an evil companion.

This verse was said by Arahant Cakkhupāla.

The Verse of Arahant Khaṇḍasumana

96. I offered just one flower. As a result I enjoyed heavenly happiness for eight hundred million years. Through the remainder of that merit, the fire of defilements has been extinguished by me.

This verse was said by Arahant Khaṇḍasumana.

The Verse of Arahant Tissa

97. I was able to give up the beautifully carved, very valuable golden bowl. Then I took a clay bowl. This is my second crowning.

This verse was said by Arahant Tissa.

The Verse of Arahant Abhaya

98. After seeing a form with the eye, if one's mindfulness is muddled he will think about its beautiful signs. He feels it with an attached mind and his mind stays clinging to that form. Then taints which lead to the origination and continuation of existence increase in him.

This verse was said by Arahant Abhaya.

The Verse of Arahant Uttiya

99. After hearing a sound with the ear, if one's mindfulness is muddled he will think about its beautiful signs. He feels it with an attached mind and his mind stays clinging to that sound. Then taints which lead to the origination and continuation of existence increase in him.

This verse was said by Arahant Uttiya.

The Verse of Arahant Devasabha

100. He practices the Dhamma with four kinds of striving. His mind is focused on the Four Establishments of Mindfulness. He

is decorated with the flowers of liberation. He will attain final extinguishing at passing away without taints.

This verse was said by Arahant Devasabha.

The Verse of Arahant Belaṭṭhakāni

101. Even though one gave up the household life and became a monk, if one doesn't follow the Dhamma path and fills one's stomach by eating too much with a mouth like a plough, that lazy one's life is like that of a bloated pig. This fool surely comes to be born in a womb again and again.

This verse was said by Arahant Belaṭṭhakāni.

The Verse of Arahant Setuccha.

102. Deceived by conceit, defiled by formations, and invaded by gains and losses, that person can never attain one-pointedness of mind.

This verse was said by Arahant Setuccha.

The Verse of Arahant Bandhura

103. I don't need sensual pleasures. I am pleased and delighted by the flavour of the Dhamma. Having drunk the best drink, the sweetest drink, the drink of sweet Dhamma, I will never taste the poison of sensual pleasures again.

This verse was said by Arahant Bandhura.

The Verse of Arahant Khitaka

104. Truly my body is very light. My mind feels a great joy and happiness. My body floats in the sky as if it were cotton blown by the wind.

This verse was said by Arahant Khitaka.

The Verse of Arahant Malitavambha

105. When I practice the Dhamma, there are times when I become lazy. But I will never get attached to sensual pleasures. If my mind desires such things, I will take my mind away from that object very quickly. I don't want to live doing unbeneficial things. Considering wisely, I enter the Dhamma path again and again.

This verse was said by Arahant Malitavambha.

The Verse of Arahant Suhemanta

106. The meanings of this Dhamma are varied with various terms and features. The one who understands only one of them has a little wisdom. But the one who understands all terms and features is a very wise person.

This verse was said by Arahant Suhemanta.

The Verse of Arahant Dhammasava

107. After considering wisely the danger of sensual pleasures, and the benefit of giving them up, I renounced the household life and became a monk. Now I have attained the Triple Knowledge. The Buddha's path has been fully followed by me.

This verse was said by Arahant Dhammasava.

The Verse of Arahant Dhammasava's Father

108. At the age of one hundred and twenty I became a monk in the Buddha's path. I too attained the Triple Knowledge. The Buddha's path has been fully followed by me.

This verse was said by Arahant Dhammasava's father.

The Verse of Arahant Saṅgharakkhita

109. This monk belongs to the Dhamma path of the most compassionate Supreme Buddha, doesn't he? He lives in solitude. But it

seems like he is not taking this Dhamma practice seriously. Yes, he is still in an ordinary condition, like a young doe in the forest.

This verse was said by Arahant Saṅgharakkhita.

The Verse of Arahant Usabha

110. The trees on the mountain tops have shot up after the fresh rain has poured over them. When Usabha sees well grown trees, he is joyful. He likes the solitude which is created by the forest.

This verse was said by Arahant Usabha.

The Verse of Arahant Jenta

111. Truly the life of a monk is hard. Household life is also hard. The Dhamma is profound. Wealth is hard to obtain. Our lives, maintained by whatever is given, are very hard. Therefore, it is fitting to think always of impermanence.

This verse was said by Arahant Jenta.

The Verse of Arahant Vacchagotta

112. I too attained the Triple Knowledge. I experienced the amazing bliss of Jhāna. I was skilled at calming the mind. I achieved the enlightenment. The Buddha's path has been fully followed by me.

This verse was said by Arahant Vacchagotta.

The Verse of Arahant Vanavaccha

113. In that forest the clear water is very beautiful. There is also a huge flat rock surrounded by monkeys and deer. That rocky mountain covered with oozing moss delights me.

This verse was said by Arahant Vanavaccha.

The Verse of Arahant Adhimutta

114. If one is greedy for bodily happiness and always spends time nourishing the body unnecessarily, how could he achieve the perfection of the monkhood when this life is fading away?

This verse was said by Arahant Adhimutta.

The Verse of Arahant Mahānāma

115.Mahānāma, you live in this mountain with lots of rocky boulders and many sāla trees. But still you couldn't tame your mind. Are you going to fail even on this famous Nesāda Mountain with shady trees?

This verse was said by Arahant Mahānāma.

The Verse of Arahant Pārāsariya

116. I gave up the desire for the six organs of contact, guarded the sense doors, and restrained my life well. Having thrown up all the defilements that generate suffering, I attained enlightenment.

This verse was said by Arahant Pārāsariya.

The Verse of Arahant Yasa

117. In those days I always applied makeup and perfumes on my body. I wore valuable clothes and decorated myself with various jewellery. But now I have attained the Triple Knowledge. The Buddha's path has been fully followed by me.

This verse was said by Arahant Yasa.

The Verse of Arahant Kimbila

118. This youth will fall down just as an unbalanced object falls down. Yes, this form appears to belong to someone else. I don't have any desire for this form. I investigate wisely the true nature of my life like looking at something that belongs to someone else.

This verse was said by Arahant Kimbila.

The Verse of Arahant Vajjiputta

119. When you go to the foot of a tree in the forest, put only Nibbāna in your heart. Dear Gotama, meditate. Don't be heedless. What is the use of that crazy hullabaloo of birds for you?

This verse was said by Arahant Vajjiputta.

The Verse of Arahant Isidatta

120. I understood the suffering of the five aggregates of clinging completely. Therefore, now only aggregates with the roots cut off remain. I have obtained the destruction of all suffering, Nibbāna. I achieved enlightenment.

This verse was said by Arahant Isidatta.

Section of Two Verses

The Verses of Arahant Uttara

121. No existence is permanent. No formation is everlasting. Again and again your five aggregates of clinging will arise and cease repeatedly.

122. I realized this danger. I don't need anything that belongs to existence. I am detached from all sensual pleasures. I achieved enlightenment.

These verses were said by Arahant Uttara.

The Verses of Arahant Piṇḍolabhāradvāja

123. This life doesn't continue without food, but food does not produce peace for the heart. Food just helps to sustain the body. Having understood this fact, I go on my alms round.

124. Superior people such as Buddhas considered the gain and homage that came to them from families to be like a pile of mud. Desire for such things is like a fine dart that is hard to pull out. Inferior people never give up gains and honours.

These verses were said by Arahant Piṇḍolabhāradvāja.

The Verses of Arahant Valliya

125. There is a cage with five doors. In that cage, there is a monkey. From time to time this monkey looks out of each door to gain contact with the outside world.

126. Hey monkey! Stand still! Do not run! Now your cage is not how it used to be. With restrained faculties and developed wis-

dom you have been controlled now. From now on you can't journey in this saṁsāra anymore.

These verses were said by Arahant Valliya.

The Verses of Arahant Gaṅgātīrya

127. I live on the bank of the Ganges River. There my hut is made out of three palm leaves. My bowl is like a funeral pot which is used to sprinkle water on dead bodies. I wear rag robes.

128. For two years I only spoke one word. In the third year after I became a monk, I split and destroyed the darkness of ignorance.

These verses were said by Arahant Gaṅgātīrya.

The Verses of Arahant Ajina

129. If one achieves the Triple Knowledge, he is a person who has ended death and eradicated all taints. But foolish people who don't know the significance of this noble person despise him by saying he's not famous.

130. But if a certain person in this world receives delicious food and drink, even though his life is evil, foolish people still honour that person.

These verses were said by Arahant Ajina.

The Verses of Arahant Meḷajina

131. From the very first day I heard the Buddha teaching this excellent Dhamma, I am not aware of having any doubt in the All-seeing, Unconquered Buddha.

132. The Supreme Buddha is the great Caravan Leader who helps beings cross over saṁsāra. I don't have any doubt in the Great Hero, the best tamer among teachers who tame others. I don't have any doubt in the excellent path or the training leading to Nibbāna.

These verses were said by Arahant Meḷajina.

The Verses of Arahant Rādha

133. Just as the rain penetrates a badly roofed house, so desire penetrates an undeveloped mind.

134. Just as the rain cannot penetrate a well roofed house, so desire cannot penetrate a well-developed mind.

These verses were said by Arahant Rādha.

The Verses of Arahant Surādha

135. My rebirth is now destroyed. The great victor's instruction has been fully followed by me. I have eradicated the ignorance that is like a net covering one's eyes. Craving that binds one to future existence is uprooted.

136. Abandoning household life, I became a monk in the Buddha's path, expecting a great goal. That goal, the perfect realization of the true nature of life, Nibbāna has been achieved by me. All fetters are eradicated.

These verses were said by Arahant Surādha.

The Verses of Arahant Gotama

137. Sages sleep very peacefully since they are not attached to women. Truly these women, who always should be guarded, tell true words very rarely.

138. Hey! Desire for sensual pleasures! We have destroyed you. Now we are not in your debt. Now we are going to Supreme Nibbāna where, having gone, one does not grieve.

These verses were said by Arahant Gotama.

The Verses of Arahant Vasabha

139. An evil person first harms himself then harms others. There is a hunter who has a bird named Vitaṁsa. Using his own bird, this hunter lures other birds. Having first been harmed, it then harms others.

140. One doesn't become a Brāhmin just by outer appearance. One becomes a true Brāhmin through good inner qualities. God Sakka! If evil deeds are seen in one's life, one is truly an evil person.

These verses were said by Arahant Vasabha.

The Verses of Arahant Mahācunda

141. In one who desires to listen to the Dhamma, knowledge of Dhamma increases. His wisdom grows through that knowledge of Dhamma. Reality can be understood through that wisdom. Realizing the truth brings true happiness.

142. One should live in remote and solitary monasteries. One should practice the Dhamma with the intention of freeing oneself from the bondage of saṁsāra. But if one doesn't like to live in a forest far away, guarding his faculties well and establishing mindfulness well, one should live under respected senior monks.

These verses were said by Arahant Mahācunda.

The Verses of Arahant Jotidāsa

143. There are some cruel people who kill others brutally, beating their heads and punishing them severely. These cruel people are the ones that will suffer. The results of bad kamma will not just disappear without ripening.

144. Whatever good or evil action a person does and accumulates, he inherits the result of that action.

These verses were said by Arahant Jotidāsa.

The Verses of Arahant Heraññakāni

145. Days and nights pass by very quickly. Life will come to an end very soon. The lives of people are reaching an end like the water of small streams.

146. But foolish evil doers don't understand this. In the end, they will have to suffer. Truly the result of evil action is also very evil.

These verses were said by Arahant Heraññakāni.

The Verses of Arahant Somamitta

147. Just as one climbing on to a small piece of wood would sink in the great ocean, even so one who lives a virtuous life sinks in saṁsāra if he associates with a lazy person. Therefore one should avoid those who are lazy and have little energy.

148. There are wise noble ones who meditate in solitary places, practise the Dhamma with great effort, develop Jhānas, and strive all the time energetically. One should associate with such wise ones.

These verses were said by Arahant Somamitta.

The Verses of Arahant Sabbamitta

149. People are bound to people by craving. People associate with the same people. People are hurt by the same people. Those people hurt other people.

150. Those people who are born from people are useless to me. Therefore, I will leave all these people and the lust and hate that trouble them. I will go towards Nibbāna.

These verses were said by Arahant Sabbamitta.

The Verses of Arahant Mahākāla

151. Her name is Kāli. Her fat body is the same color as a crow. Two thighs of her dead body were stuck together. Two hand of her dead body were also stuck together. The split head of her dead body is like a curds-bowl.

152. Only an ignorant person would have a desire for this body. That fool comes to pain again and again. Therefore, one who

understands this reality doesn't have desire for this body. May I never lie again like this, with a split head.

These verses were said by Arahant Mahākāla.

The Verses of Arahant Tissa

153. When a monk with a shaved head, wearing a double robe gains plenty of food, drink, robes and shelter, he also gains a lot of enemies at the same time.

154. Seeing this danger, the wise monk is afraid of honours. So, little gain is good enough. Then he will live mindfully without increasing defilements.

These verses were said by Arahant Tissa.

The Verses of Arahant Kimbila

155. That forest is called Pacinavaṁsa. There is a group of companion monks of the Sākya clan in that forest. They became monks having given up great wealth. They practice the Dhamma with delight, being happy eating whatever they receive on their alms round.

156. Those monks are very energetic, extremely energetic. Dhamma practise is their first priority. Their own life is the second. Having given up worldly enjoyment, they delight in spiritual enjoyment connected to Dhamma practice.

These verses were said by Arahant Kimbila.

The Verses of Arahant Nanda

157. Those days I followed a wrong thinking pattern. I was addicted to decorating my body. My mind was not peaceful because it was filled with obsession and sensual lust. I was conceited.

158. But the Supreme Buddha, the kinsman of the sun, is very strategic. With the help of the Buddha, I started to wisely investi-

gate the truth. I was firm in the practice. My mind was drowning in existence: I pulled it out. I lifted my mind up towards Nibbāna.

These verses were said by Arahant Nanda.

The Verses of Arahant Sirimanta

159. It doesn't matter how much others praise someone who doesn't have a still mind. That praise is worthless because that person's mind is not still.

160. It doesn't matter how much others blame someone who does have a perfectly still mind. That blame is worthless because that person's mind is perfectly still.

These verses were said by Arahant Sirimanta.

The Verses of Arahant Uttara

161. I understood the suffering of the five aggregates of clinging completely. My craving has been completely rooted out. The Enlightenment Factors have been developed by me. I have attained enlightenment.

162. Because I completely understood the suffering of the five aggregates of clinging, craving has been completely rooted out and the Enlightenment Factors have been developed by me. I will attain final extinguishing at passing away without taints.

These verses were said by Arahant Uttara.

The Verses of Arahant Bhaddaji

163. That king was called Panāda. He had a golden mansion. Its height was two hundred and fifty kilometers. Its width was five kilometers.

164. The mansion had a thousand roofs with flags on each of them. In the mansion six thousand dancers were always dancing. I was king Panāda at that time.

These verses were said by Arahant Bhaddaji.

The Verses of Arahant Sobhita

165. I'm a very energetic, wise and mindful monk. I could recollect five hundred eons back like I recollect one night.

166. I developed the Four Establishments of Mindfulness, the Seven Enlightenment Factors and the Noble Eightfold Path. That is why I could recollect five hundred eons back like I recollect one night.

These verses were said by Arahant Sobhita.

The Verses of Arahant Valliya

167. What is to be done by one with strong energy to gain enlightenment, that I will definitely do. I will not miss it. See my energy and effort!

168. Bhante, teach me the straight path that leads to Nibbāna. I too will reach that Nibbāna, the goal of the sages, by following the sages' path, like the stream of a river quickly flowing into the ocean.

These verses were said by Arahant Valliya.

The Verses of Arahant Vītasoka

169. That day the barber approached me to shave my head. Then, taking the mirror, I looked at my body.

170. My body appeared to be something empty. The darkness of ignorance is abandoned. Rags of ignorance have been torn out. There is no more rebirth for me.

These verses were said by Arahant Vītasoka.

The Verses of Arahant Puṇṇamāsa

171. I abandoned the five hindrances. I took the Mirror of Dhamma, the knowledge of insight, only with the intention of attaining Nibbāna.

172. Using that Mirror of Dhamma, I investigated this life inside and out. Both inside and outside of this life seemed empty to me.

These verses were said by Arahant Puṇṇamāsa.

The Verses of Arahant Nandaka

173. Just as the best type of noble ox, having stumbled, stands firm again with a deep sense of urgency, with great determination, he continues to carry heavy loads on his back.

174. So too should you consider me as the best type of person possessed of noble insight, a disciple of the fully enlightened Buddha. Consider me as the Buddha's son born from the Blessed One's heart.

These verses were said by Arahant Nandaka.

The Verses of Arahant Bharata

175. Come dear Nandaka, let us go into the presence of the preceptor, the Great Teacher, the Supreme Buddha. Let's roar the lion's roar in the presence of the Buddha.

176. Out of compassion, the Buddha ordained us in order to give a great thing. We have achieved that great goal. All fetters that bind us to saṁsāra have been eradicated.

These verses were said by Arahant Bharata.

The Verses of Arahant Bhāradvāja

177. Sages are like the lions who roar in the mountain caves; they are very wise and energetic. They defeated Māra and his army. They roar a lion's roar because they won the battle over defilements.

178. The Great Teacher's instruction has been respectfully followed by me. I was able to respect the Dhamma and the Saṅgha.

When I see the Supreme Buddha's sons free from defilements, my heart is filled with spiritual joy.

These verses were said by Arahant Bhāradvāja.

The Verses of Arahant Kaṇhadinna

179. I was fortunate enough to associate with superior people and to listen to the Dhamma frequently. Since I lived according to the Dhamma I heard, I entered the path to Nibbāna.

180. I live constantly with mindfulness. Desire for rebirth was eradicated by me. Desire for existence will never arise in me again. From the day I realized the Dhamma, I didn't have any defilements. They will not arise in the future. In the present too, they are not found in me. I know this very well.

These verses were said by Arahant Kaṇhadinna.

The Verses of Arahant Migasira

181. Since I became a monk in the Buddha's path, cleansing my mind from defilements, I rose up. I overcame the sensual realm.

182. One day the Supreme Buddha, possessed of the Four Divine Abodes, was looking at me. At that moment my mind was liberated from all defilements. My liberation is unshakeable. All fetters are eradicated.

These verses were said by Arahant Migasira.

The Verses of Arahant Sīvaka

183. The house of saṁsāra that is built again and again in this existence is impermanent. I should discover that house builder. Rebirth again and again is painful.

184. Hey house builder! I have seen you! You will not be able to build a house for me again. I have broken all of the rafters in the

house you have built. The center beam is split and destroyed. The mind, made free of boundaries will cease in this very life.

These verses were said by Arahant Sīvaka.

The Verses of Arahant Upavāna

185. The greatest Arahant, the follower of the Noble Path, our Great Sage, the Buddha, is sick, troubled by winds. Brāhmin, if there is hot water; please give it to me for my Great Sage.

186. Our Great Sage is honoured by those who are to be honoured, revered by those who are to be revered, respected by those who are to be respected. I truly wish for my Great Sage's recovery.

These verses were said by Arahant Upavāna.

The Verses of Arahant Isidinna

187. I have seen some lay followers who are experts in the Dhamma. They say, "Sensual pleasures are impermanent," but they cling to jewellery, wives and children. They wish for them again and again.

188. Truly these lay followers don't know the Dhamma as it really is. Even though they say, "Sensual pleasures are impermanent," they have no power to cut off their desire. Because of that they are mingled with children, wives and wealth.

These verses were said by Arahant Isidinna.

The Verses of Arahant Sambulakaccāna

189. It is raining. The water flows with a musical sound. I am alone in this fearful cave. Even though I am alone in that fearful cave, I don't have any fear, terror, or hair raising at all.

190. When I live in this fearful cave alone, I do not have any fear, terror or hair raising at all because fearlessness is a natural law in my life.

These verses were said by Arahant Sambulakaccāna.

The Verses of Arahant Khitaka

191. Whose mind is still and unshaken like a rocky mountain? Whose mind is unattached to lustful objects? Whose mind is not irritated at irritated objects? If one has developed his mind in the Dhamma like this, how could suffering come to him?

192. My mind is still and unshaken like a rocky mountain. My mind is unattached to lustful object. My mind is not irritated at irritating objects. My mind has been developed in the Dhamma to this stage. So how could suffering come to me?

These verses were said by Arahant Khitaka.

The Verses of Arahant Selissariya

193. Garlands of stars shine in this delightful night. It's not yet the time to sleep. This night is ideal to meditate without sleeping for those who see the true nature of this life.

194. That day when I fell down from the back of the elephant, if it had stepped on me, I wouldn't have been living today. But death would be better for me than to live, having been defeated in battle with the defilements.

These verses were said by Arahant Selissariya.

The Verses of Arahant Nisabha

195. The one who becomes a monk out of faith, having given up house and sensual pleasures that are delightful and pleasing to the mind, can end this suffering.

196. I don't long for death. I don't long for life. With clear mindfulness and awareness I am awaiting the day to attain final extinguishing at passing away.

These verses were said by Arahant Nisabha.

The Verses of Arahant Usabha

197. I had a very strange dream. I was wearing a robe that had the colour of a young mango leaf. I went to the village to beg for food while sitting on the back of an elephant.

198. I felt ashamed and agitated in the midst of people. As soon as I got off the elephant, I woke up. At that time I felt a great shame. Those days I was intoxicated with conceit. But now I have attained enlightenment.

These verses were said by Arahant Usabha.

The Verses of Arahant Kappaṭakura

199. This Kappaṭakura monk still thinks about rags. He is on the bank of deathlessness. He is a monk just for the name. But he is able to attain Jhānas well.

200. Dear Kappaṭakura, don't try to sleep like that. May your cheek not get hit by this hand. Dear Kappaṭa, you sleep in the midst of the Saṅgha; you don't even know the limit of sleeping.

These verses were said by Arahant Kappaṭakura.

The Verses of Arahant Kumārakassapa

201. Truly Supreme Buddhas are amazing. This excellent Dhamma is amazing. The guidance of this greatest teacher is amazing. That is why disciples have the chance to realize this excellent Dhamma.

202. I have obtained this life of five aggregates of clinging for innumerable eons. Among all these lives, only this has become the last. This is my final body. There is no more rebirth for me in this cycle of birth and death.

These verses were said by Arahant Kumārakassapa.

The Verses of Arahant Dhammapāla

203. There is a young monk who follows the Buddha's path very energetically. He practices meditation diligently. When the whole world is sleeping, he isn't. He meditates in the night. His life is not in vain.

204. Therefore, a wise monk is faithful, virtuous and confident in the Triple Gem. He realizes this Dhamma. That is why he strives hard recollecting the Buddha's message.

These verses were said by Arahant Dhammapāla.

The Verses of Arahant Brahmāli

205. Who has calmed faculties like a horse well tamed by a charioteer? Who has an unagitated, taintless and pride-free mind? Who do even the gods adore?

206. I have calmed faculties like a horse well tamed by a charioteer. I have an unagitated, taintless and pride-free mind. Even the gods adore me.

These verses were said by Arahant Brahmāli.

The Verses of Arahant Mogharāja

207. The colour of his skin is not beautiful but he has a beautiful mind. Dear Mogharāja, you have a perfectly calm mind. Being a monk, how did you spend the cold dark nights in winter?

208. I have heard that all the people of Magadha province have plenty of rice. So, like other people who live in comfort, I spend the nights in a straw hut.

These verses were said by Arahant Mogharāja.

The Verses of Arahant Visākha Pañcālaputta

209. He doesn't exalt himself nor does he put others down. He doesn't go against enlightened ones. He doesn't praise himself in

the assemblies. He is not agitated. He speaks knowing the limit. He has good behavior.

210. Noble senior monks are obedient to the Dhamma. They understand very profound and subtle meanings of the Dhamma. They are very skilled in gaining wisdom. For a monk who associates with such noble monks, it is not hard to achieve Nibbāna.

These verses were said by Arahant Visākha Pañcālaputta.

The Verses of Arahant Cūḷaka

211. Those peacocks' necks are blue. They have beautiful tail feathers. Their beaks are also beautiful. They sing beautiful songs. This great earth is well covered in grass. The blue flowing water is very beautiful. The clouds in this sky are also very beautiful.

212. The life of one with a beautiful mind is also like this. Therefore, meditate. How wonderful is it to be liberated from defilements based upon the Buddha's path? One should experience the most pure, subtle, and very hard to see Nibbāna.

These verses were said by Arahant Cūḷaka.

The Verses of Arahant Anūpama

213. This mind has wondered on a long journey seeking happiness in existence. The mind is as if standing on a spear. Without any benefit, this mind is attached where there is the spear of suffering.

214. I call you "witch mind"! I call you "rogue mind"! Now you have met the greatest teacher who is hard to find. Now do not take me on the wrong path.

These verses were said by Arahant Anūpama.

The Verses of Arahant Vajjita

215. For a long time I have been journeying in this saṁsāra through good worlds and bad worlds. It was because I was a blind

ordinary person without an understanding of the Four Noble Truths.

216. But by practicing the Dhamma diligently, the journey of saṁsāra was brought to an end. Journey through good and bad worlds is cut out completely. There is no more rebirth for me.

These verses were said by Arahant Vajjita.

The Verses of Arahant Sanbhita

217. That well grown fig tree was full of green leaves. I meditated at the foot of that tree. There, mindfully I developed the perception of the recollection of the qualities of the Supreme Buddha.

218. I practised that very same perception thirty-one eons ago. By using the same meditation, I was able to attain enlightenment.

These verses were said by Arahant Sanbhita.

Section of Three Verses

The Verses of Arahant Aggikabhāradvāja

219. Seeking purity in the wrong way, I was offering fire sacrifices in the forest. Not knowing the path to Nibbāna, I practiced various austerities. But they did not benefit me in any way.

220. But see the excellence of the Dhamma! I achieved the Supreme bliss of Nibbāna through a happy path. I achieved the Triple Knowledge, the Buddha's path has been fully followed by me.

221. Previously, I was a Brāhmin just in name. But now I am a true Brāhmin. I possess the Triple Knowledge. Washing away defilements, I have reached the goodness, the culmination of the Dhamma practice.

These verses were said by Arahant Aggikabhāradvāja.

The Verses of Arahant Paccaya

222. It was only five days since I became a monk and still was a trainee. So I went into the hut and made a determination like this:

223. "Until I remove the dart of craving, I won't eat anything. I won't drink anything. I won't leave my hut and I won't sleep leaning my body on any side."

224. See how energetic I was! I was striving hard. I achieved the Triple Knowledge. The Buddha's path has been fully followed by me.

These verses were said by Arahant Paccaya.

The Verses of Arahant Bakkula

225. If one thinks to do things later that should've been done before, he will miss the chance to gain happiness. He will be remorseful later.

226. One should say only what one will do; one should not say what one will not do. Wise people do not praise those who talk but don't act as they speak.

227. Nibbāna, taught by the Supreme Buddha, is truly the highest happiness. Suffering ceases only there. In Nibbāna there is no sorrow or defilements. True assurance is in Nibbāna.

These verses were said by Arahant Bakkula.

The Verses of Arahant Dhaniya

228. A monk who wishes to improve his monk life and wants to live happily should not despise the robes, food, and drink given to the community of monks.

229. A monk who wishes to improve his monk life and wants to live happily should use a shelter with the idea of temporary use, just like a snake slithers into a mouse's hole.

230. A monk who wishes to improve his monk life and wants to live happily should be content with whatever is given. The single best quality should be cultivated: Diligent practice of the Dhamma.

These verses were said by Arahant Dhaniya.

The Verses of Arahant Mātaṅgaputta

231. Saying "Now it is too cold", "Now it is too hot", and "Now it is too late in the evening," some people become negligent and lose the opportunity for improvement in their occupation. These people will also miss this very rare opportunity.

232. One should ignore cold and heat as if they were grass. If one strives with manly energy, one will not lose happiness.

233. I push through dabba grass, kusa grass, potakila grass, usīra grass, muñja grass and bulrushes. I devote myself to seclusion.

These verses were said by Arahant Mātaṅgaputta.

The Verses of Arahant Khujjasobhita

234. Pāṭaliputta is a great city where good recluses live. They can preach very beautifully. They have a vast knowledge of the Dhamma. The monk Khujjasobhita, standing at the door of the monastery, is one of those good recluses.

235. Pāṭaliputta is a great city where good recluses live. They can preach very beautifully. They have a vast knowledge of the Dhamma. The monk Khujjasobhita is one of those good recluses and he came near the door using his psychic powers, as if blown by the wind.

236. Destroying defilements is called a good war. Cultivating good qualities is called a good sacrifice. Having won the battle of defilements, having practised this holy life, he experiences true happiness.

These verses were said by Arahant Khujjasobhita.

The Verses of Arahant Vāraṇa

237. Whoever among humans kills beings, declines in this world and the next.

238. But whoever with a mind of loving kindness has pity on all living beings, such a person collects a lot of merit.

239. One should learn this well-preached Dhamma. One should associate with great recluses. That person always lives in solitude and trains in calming the mind.

These verses were said by Arahant Vāraṇa.

The Verses of Arahant Passika

240. If there is one faithful and wise person among unfaithful relatives, because of that virtuous person who is established in the Dhamma, all his relatives benefit.

241. I rebuked and warned my relatives truly out of compassion. Because of their love for me as a relative, they followed my advice. They started serving the monks.

242. After passing away, my mother and brother were reborn in heaven. Now they live very happily receiving whatever happiness they wish.

These verses were said by Arahant Passika.

The Verses of Arahant Yasoja

243. That person's limbs are like the knots of black vines. He is very thin with his veins showing. But he knows the purpose of eating and drinking. His mind is victorious.

244. He goes into the middle of the thick forest to meditate. There mosquitos and flies surround and attack him. He endures those attacks with clear mindfulness like a king elephant in the battlefield.

245. Living alone is like a Brahma. Two people living together are like gods. Three people living together are like a village. More than that is definitely a quarrel.

These verses were said by Arahant Yasoja.

The Verses of Arahant Sāṭimattiya

246. Previously, you had faith in me but today it is different. You don't have that faith anymore. Whatever done by you is yours. Such bad conduct as you think is not found in me.

247. Ordinary people's faith is truly impermanent. It changes in a moment. I have seen it clearly. Sometimes they show faith and

are pleased. But other times, they lose faith and are displeased. Would a sage get upset because of that? Of course not.

248. In this house and that, a little bit of rice here and there is cooked for a sage. Therefore, I survive on my alms round and still have strength in my legs.

These verses were said by Arahant Sātimattiya.

The Verses of Arahant Upāli

249. A newly ordained monk who entered the Buddha's path out of faith, abandoning the home life, should practice right livelihood. He should be energetic and associate with noble friends.

250. A newly ordained monk who entered the Buddha's path out of faith, abandoning the home life, should live in the midst of monks. He should learn the code of conduct well.

251. A newly ordained monk who entered the Buddha's path out of faith, abandoning the home life, should be skilled in recognising what is allowable and unallowable. He should live without focusing on craving.

These verses were said by Arahant Upāli.

The Verses of Arahant Uttarapāla

252. While I was indeed very clever to understand what is good and bad, still five cords of sensual pleasures that make the world deluded caused me to fall down.

253. Sensual pleasures are the place where Māra traps beings. I too was trapped by these sensual pleasures. I was hit by the dart of lust. But finally I was able to free my life from the snare of Māra.

254. I have eliminated all sensual pleasures. All existence has been destroyed. Journeying on from rebirth to rebirth in saṁsāra has been put to an end. There is no more rebirth for me.

These verses were said by Arahant Uttarapāla.

The Verses of Arahant Abhibhūta

255. Dear relatives, as many as are assembled here, listen to what I am going to say. I will teach you the Supreme Buddha's Dhamma. Rebirth again and again is very painful.

256. Therefore, strive energetically. Get rid of laziness. Follow the instruction of the Supreme Buddha. Knock down the army of Māra as a king elephant knocks down a bamboo hut.

257. Whoever practices this Dhamma heedfully, eliminating journeying from rebirth to rebirth puts an end to all suffering.

These verses were said by Arahant Abhibhūta.

The Verses of Arahant Gotama

258. While journeying on in this saṁsāra, I was reborn in hell again and again. I was reborn in the hungry ghost world. I was reborn in the animal world. For a long time I suffered a lot.

259. From time to time I was reborn in the human world too. From time to time I was reborn in heaven as well. I was reborn in fine material and non-material brahma worlds. Time passed by being born in the neither-percipient nor impercipient world and in the impercipient world.

260. Now I know the arising of all formations is meaningless. All conditioned things are vulnerable to destruction. With developed wisdom I realised the true nature of all conditioned things that I considered to be mine. Establishing mindfulness well, I attained peaceful Nibbāna.

These verses were said by Arahant Gotama.

The Verses of Arahant Hārita

261. If one thinks to do things later that should've been done before he will miss the chance to gain happiness. He will be remorseful later.

262. One should say only what one would do; one should not say what one will not do. Wise people do not praise those who talk but don't act as they speak.

263. Nibbāna, taught by the Supreme Buddha, is truly the highest happiness. Suffering ceases only there. In Nibbāna there is no sorrow or defilements. True assurance is in Nibbāna.

These verses were said by Arahant Hārita.

The Verses of Arahant Vimala

264. One who wishes to attain Nibbāna should avoid evil friends, associate with noble people and follow their advice.

265. Just as one climbing onto a small piece of wood would sink in the great ocean, so, even a virtuous person's good qualities deteriorate if he associates with a lazy person. Therefore one should avoid lazy and unenergetic people.

266. One should associate with noble people who live alone, practice the Dhamma as a top priority; practice Jhānas, and continually put forth energy.

These verses were said by Arahant Vimala.

Section of Four Verses

The Verses of Arahant Nāgasamāla

267. She was a dancing girl. She was beautifully dressed, decorated with ornaments and wearing flower garlands. Her whole body was covered with sandalwood cream. In the middle of the main road she was dancing to music.

268. At that time I entered the main road for my alms round. As I was going alone, I saw her, beautifully dressed and decorated with ornaments. It occurred to me that she was like a snare put out by Māra.

269. Based on this incident, I gained wise consideration. I started to think wisely. The danger of sensual pleasures was clear to me. Disenchantment with life was established in my mind.

270. Based on this same incident, my mind was liberated from all defilements. See the excellence of this Dhamma! I too attained the Triple Knowledge. The Buddha's path has been fully followed by me.

These verses were said by Arahant Nāgasamāla.

The Verses of Arahant Bhagu

271. I was very sleepy. I came out of my hut still sleepy. I stepped on the walking path to practice walking meditation. I fell to the ground on that very spot.

272. I got up, rubbed my arms and legs and stepped on the walking path again. However, I managed to practice walking meditation. I was able to still my mind.

273. Based on this incident, I gained wise consideration. I started to think wisely. The danger of sensual pleasures was clear to me. Disenchantment with life was established in my mind.

274. Based on this same incident, my mind was liberated from all defilements. See the excellence of this Dhamma! I too attained the Triple Knowledge. The Buddha's path has been fully followed by me.

These verses were said by Arahant Bhagu.

The Verses of Arahant Sabhiya

275. Many people don't know that we all will die one day. But if one understands that he will die one day, his quarrels would come to an end.

276. Those who don't understand this reality live like they will never die. But if one understands this reality, he will live freed from getting sick with defilements among the people who are sick with defilements.

277. Through slacking practice, defiled observances, and impure celibacy one can't get a great benefit.

278. If one doesn't have respect toward his fellow monks, he is as far from the true Dhamma as the sky is from the earth.

These verses were said by Arahant Sabhiya.

The Verses of Arahant Nandaka

279. Your body is filled with filth. It has a terrible smell. It is on Māra's side. You woman, oozing with defilements, curse on you. Your body has nine doors. Filth is oozing from each door all the time.

280. Don't try to be funny with me like before. Don't offend the disciples of the Buddha. They are not even interested in heavenly happiness let alone human happiness.

281. But those who are fools are stupid and cloaked in delusion. Only such slacking people are interested in those things. They all are caught in the snare of Māra.

282. Those who have discarded desire, hatred and ignorance, and have unagitated minds are not interested in those things. They have cut the cord of craving; therefore they are not attached to sensual pleasures.

These verses were said by Arahant Nandaka.

The Verses of Arahant Jambuka

283. For fifty-five years, I didn't wear anything at all. I covered my body with dust. I only ate one meal a month, putting a very small quantity of rice on my tongue. I ripped out my beard and hair.

284. I rejected seats; I stood on one leg. I ate dry dung and I did not accept any invitations.

285. In this way, I collected a lot of demerit leading to a bad destination. While I was drowning in the great flood of defilements, I was able to go for refuge to the Supreme Buddha.

286. See the assurance of my arrival to the Noble Triple Gem! See the excellence of the Dhamma! I achieved the Triple Knowledge. The Buddha's path has been fully followed by me.

These verses were said by Arahant Jambuka.

The Verses of Arahant Senaka

287. I came to the beach of Gayā to see an auspicious festival. Truly, I had gone to the correct place. That day I saw the Supreme Buddha teaching the excellent Dhamma.

288. The Buddha's life is bright with great wisdom. He is an excellent teacher for all disciples, and the foremost in all the three worlds. The Buddha is the leader of all three worlds and the greatest sage of gods and humans. Even the sight of the Buddha is incredible.

289. The Supreme Buddha is like a great king elephant. He is a great hero. He is glorious. Having destroyed all taints, the Buddha lives without taints. I saw my Great Teacher, the one who doesn't have any fear at all.

290. Previously, I was defiled with various views and opinions. But the Blessed One freed this Senaka from all ties of defilements.

These verses were said by Arahant Senaka.

The Verses of Arahant Sambhūta

291. The fool hurries when it is time to be patient, and he is patient when it is time to hurry. Having followed the wrong way, he finally comes to pain.

292. His success declines like the moon in the dark fortnight. He acquires disgrace. His friends act against him.

293. The wise one is patient when it is time to be patient, and he hurries when it is time to hurry. Having followed the right way, he finally comes to happiness.

294. His success increases like the moon in the bright fortnight. He acquires fame. His good friends don't act against him.

These verses were said by Arahant Sambhūta.

The Verses of Arahant Rāhula

295. I was fortunate to be Prince Siddhārtha's son. Now I am fortunate to be the disciple-son of the Supreme Buddha. I have been fortunate to be a son in these two ways. Therefore, wise noble ones call me "lucky" Rāhula. As a disciple-son of the Supreme Buddha, I gained the eye of Dhamma.

296. My taints are eradicated. Rebirth is ended. I became an enlightened one. I am entitled to offerings and homage from people. I achieved the Triple Knowledge and attained Nibbāna, freedom from death.

297. But most people are blinded by sensual pleasures. They are enveloped in the net of defilements. They are covered with the cloak of craving. They are bound to saṁsāra by Māra, the relative of the lazy people, like a fish bound by the fisherman's net.

298. I abandoned those sensual pleasures. I cut off Māra's bonds. I uprooted craving from its roots. I have become cool and extinguished.

These verses were said by Arahant Rāhula.

The Verses of Arahant Candana

299. That day, my former wife, decorated with jewelry and ornaments, surrounded by servant girls, came up to me carrying her son upon her hip.

300. When I saw my son's mother decorated with ornaments, well dressed, coming to me, she seemed to me like a snare put by Māra.

301. Based on this incident, wise consideration arose in me. The danger of sensual pleasures was clear to me. Disenchantment with life was established in my mind.

302. Based on this same incident, my mind was liberated from all defilements. See the excellence of this Dhamma! I too attained the Triple Knowledge. The Buddha's path has been fully followed by me.

These verses were said by Arahant Candana.

The Verses of Arahant Dhammika

303. Dhamma can truly protect the one who practices it. When Dhamma is well practiced, it brings happiness. The benefit of practising the Dhamma well is this: the one who practises the Dhamma doesn't go to a bad destination.

304. Dhamma practise and wrong practise don't have equal results. Wrong practice takes beings to hell. Dhamma practice takes beings to heaven.

305. Therefore, one should desire the Good Dhamma. One should rejoice in the Dhamma of the founder of the Great Path, the one with an unshaken mind. The wise disciples with the best refuge, who stand in the Dhamma of the best teacher, can reach Nibbāna.

306. Sensual pleasures are like a wound. He uprooted the root of those sensual pleasures. He cut off the net of craving. His journey in saṁsāra is ended. He is devoid of the stain of craving like the shining moon without stains on a full moon night.

These verses were said by Arahant Dhammika.

The Verses of Arahant Sappaka

307. That crane's wings have the colour of a white lotus. She was terrified by fear of the black cloud. When she flees seeking a shelter, this river Ajakaraṇī delights my heart.

308. That crane's body has the colour of a white lotus. She was terrified of the black cloud. She doesn't have a place to hide. When she flees looking for a hiding place, this river Ajakarani delights my heart.

309. There are rose-apple trees on the two banks of the river. Who wouldn't be delighted by these trees? The rose apple trees behind my cave beautify the whole area.

310. Frogs make noises bravely. Maybe it is because they have escaped from snakes. This time of year, the rivers in the mountain are overflowing their banks. The river Ajakarani, is safe, pleasant and delightful.

These verses were said by Arahant Sappaka.

The Verses of Arahant Mudita

311. I became a monk just to survive. But after I received higher ordination, a great faith developed in me. I strived with great effort.

312. Yes, let this body be broken into parts. Let the lumps of flesh in this body dissolve. Let both my legs fall from the knee-joints.

313. Until I uproot the dart of craving I shall not eat anything; I shall not drink anything; I shall not go out of my hut, nor shall I lie down on my side.

314. I strived like that. See my great effort! I achieved the Triple Knowledge. The Buddha's path has been fully followed by me.

These verses were said by Arahant Mudita.

Section of Five Verses

The Verses of Arahant Rājadatta

315. I'm a monk. One day I went to the cemetery. I saw a women's dead body, thrown away, and full of worms. They were devouring it.

316. Normally, when people see such a nasty dead body they are disgusted. But in my case, an unusual thing happened: lust arose in me. Truly I was looking at that dead oozing body as if I was blind.

317. Quicker than the cooking of rice, I left that place. Establishing clear mindfulness and awareness, I sat down in another place.

318. Based on this incident, wise consideration arose in me. The danger of sensual pleasures was clear to me. Disenchantment with life was established in my mind.

319. Based on this same incident, my mind was liberated from all defilements. See the excellence of this Dhamma! I too attained the Triple Knowledge. The Buddha's path has been fully followed by me.

These verses were said by Arahant Rājadatta.

The Verses of Arahant Subhūta

320. He wishes for good. But he has put his life on a wrong path. No matter how hard he practices that path, he can't attain goodness. That is the mark of bad fortune.

321. Without abandoning defilements, if someone forgets that heedfulness is the only factor that leads to purification, it is a great misfortune. If someone abandons all wholesome qualities,

he won't understand what is beneficial and unbeneficial. He is a blind man.

322. One should say only what one would do; one should not say what one would not do. Wise people do not praise those who talk but don't act as they speak.

323. Even though a flower is very colourful and beautiful, without fragrance it is not complete. In the same way, the person who doesn't follow the well spoken words of the Buddha does not get good results.

324. A colourful and beautiful flower is truly valuable if it has a nice fragrance. In the same way, the person who does follow the well spoken words of the Buddha gets good results.

These verses were said by Arahant Subhūta.

The Verses of Arahant Grimānanda

325. The rain falls musically. My small hut is well roofed. The window is also closed. This is very comfortable. I live with a calm mind. Therefore, rain cloud, rain as much as you want.

326. The rain falls musically. My small hut is well roofed. The window is also closed. This is very comfortable. I live with a peaceful mind. Therefore, rain cloud, rain as much as you want.

327. The rain falls musically. My small hut is well roofed. The window is also closed. This is very comfortable. I live with a lust-free mind. Therefore, rain cloud, rain as much as you want.

328. The rain falls musically. My small hut is well roofed. The window is also closed. This is very comfortable. I live with a hate-free mind. Therefore, rain cloud, rain as much as you want.

329. The rain falls musically. My small hut is well roofed. The window is also closed. This is very comfortable. I live with a delusion-free mind. Therefore, rain cloud, rain as much as you want.

These verses were said by Arahant Grimānanda.

The Verses of Arahant Sumana

330. I wished for only one thing in this Dhamma practice. My preceptor helped with that. I desired the freedom from death, Nibbāna. I have done the task to achieve that goal.

331. I attained the supreme bliss of Nibbāna. I experienced it and went beyond all doubts about it. I announce this to you with purified knowledge and without doubt.

332. I gained the knowledge to understand my past lives. My divine eye is purified. I attained enlightenment. The Buddha's path has been fully followed by me.

333. I learned about the path to Nibbāna very well in your teaching. I developed virtue, one-pointedness and wisdom diligently. All taints have been destroyed. Now, there is no more rebirth for me.

334. You, my great teacher, taught me the Noble path. You were compassionate and very helpful to me. My great teacher, your instructions were not in vain. Now I am a well-trained pupil.

These verses were said by Arahant Sumana.

The Verses of Arahant Vaḍḍha

335. It is wonderful how my mother advised me. It was like warning me with a stick. Having listened to advice from my mother, I followed. I practised the Dhamma energetically giving it first priority. I attained supreme enlightenment.

336. Now I am an enlightened one. I am worthy of gifts. I have gained the Triple Knowledge. I have seen Nibbāna. I have conquered the army of Māra. Now I live free from taints.

337. All internal and external taints that were found in my life have been destroyed without remaining. They will never rise again.

338. My younger sister is also well skilled in the Dhamma. Confidently, she also told about this: "Defilements are not seen in you, defilements are not seen in me."

339. All suffering has been brought to an end. This is the final body. Within the cycle of birth and death there is no more rebirth for me.

These verses were said by Arahant Vaḍḍha.

The Verses of Arahant Nadī Kassapa

340. Truly for my benefit, that day the Buddha came to the bank of the river Neranjara. Having listened to the Buddha's teaching, I abandoned wrong view.

341. Previously, I lived as a foolish, blind, ordinary person. I performed various sacrifices and fire offerings thinking that was the way to purity.

342. I lived captured by wrong views. I clung to them tightly and I was deluded. I was ignorant and blind. I was mistaken, thinking impurity was purity.

343. But now, my wrong view is eradicated. I have destroyed all existences. Now I do an excellent fire sacrifice: living a life that is worthy of gifts. I worship the Tathāgatha, the Buddha.

344. All delusion has been eradicated. Craving for existence has been destroyed. Journeying on from rebirth to rebirth has completely ended. Now there is no more rebirth for me.

These verses were said by Arahant Nadī Kassapa.

The Verses of Arahant Gayā Kassapa

345. Previously, three times a day—in the morning, at midday and in the evening—I went down into the water from the bank of the Gaya Elgu River at Gaya.

346. Formerly, I held the view that whatever evil was done by me in previous births can now be washed away here.

347. Later, I got to hear the meaningful and well spoken words of the Buddha. I reflected wisely on that meaningful, true and practical Dhamma.

348. I washed away all evil with the water of Dhamma. I scrubbed away the stain of ignorance and became purified and clean. I received the pure inheritance of the pure Buddha. I became a son who was born from the heart of the Buddha.

349. Having plunged into the stream of the Noble Eightfold Path, I have washed all my evil away. I have attained the Triple Knowledge. The Buddha's path has been fully followed by me.

These verses were said by Arahant Gayā Kassapa.

The Verses of Arahant Vakkali

350. [The Blessed One:] Monk, you live in a great forest. You're suffering from an illness due to a wind disorder. You don't even receive the four requisites well. How do you live this tough life?

351. [Vakkali:] Much Joy and happiness have spread inside my body. It is because of this that I endure my tough life and live in the forest.

352. Developing the Four Establishments of Mindfulness, Five Spiritual Faculties, Five Spiritual Powers, and Seven Enlightenments Factors, I live in this forest.

353. Seeing my fellow monks who practice the Dhamma energetically, giving the training first priority, always with strong effort and living in harmony, I live in the forest.

354. Recollecting the foremost in the three worlds, the well tamed one, the perfectly still one, the Supreme Buddha, I live in the forest diligently both day and night.

These verses were said by Arahant Vakkali.

The Verses of Arahant Vijitasena

355. Hey, mind! Now I will stop you from roaming around with unnecessary thoughts. I keep you controlled like an elephant tied to the gate of the city. You, mind! Born of the body, with a net of sensual pleasures, I won't incite you to evil.

356. The gate of the city will never be opened for that elephant. That is how I restrained you from unnecessary thoughts. You, witch mind! Don't be mean! Now you should not be delighting in evil.

357. The newly caught elephant is very aggressive. When the strong elephant trainer tries to tame the elephant with a hook, the elephant unwillingly becomes tamed. That is how I am going to tame you.

358. As an excellent charioteer who is skilled in the taming of excellent horses, standing firm in Five Spiritual Powers, I will tame you.

359. Hey, mind! I have tied you with the rope called mindfulness. I will cleanse you with a purified life. Rebuking your faults, pushing you with great energy, I have restrained you from all evil. From now on, mind, you won't have any journeying in this cycle of birth and death.

These verses were said by Arahant Vijitasena.

The Verses of Arahant Yasadatta

360. The fool hears the Buddha's Dhamma with a fault-finding mind. He is as far away from the Dhamma as the earth is from the sky.

361. The fool hears the Supreme Buddha's Dhamma with a fault-finding mind. He declines from the Dhamma like the declining moon into the darkness.

362. The fool hears the Supreme Buddha's Dhamma with a fault-finding mind. He dries up in the Dhamma like a fish in little water.

363. The fool hears the Supreme Buddha's Dhamma with a fault-finding mind. He does not grow in the Dhamma like a rotten seed in a field.

364. But the wise person listens to the Supreme Buddha's Dhamma with a joyful mind. He eliminates all the taints. Having realized Nibbāna, he attains the highest peace. With a taint-free mind, he attains final extinguishing at passing away.

These verses were said by Arahant Yasadatta.

The Verses of Arahant Soṇa Kuṭikaṇṇa

365. I too obtained higher ordination. Being freed from taints, I was liberated from defilements. That day when I went to see the Blessed One, I had a great opportunity to stay the night in the same dwelling where the Buddha stayed.

366. On that occasion, the Blessed One spent much of the night outside doing walking meditation. Then our Great Teacher, who is skilled in dwelling in various meditative absorptions, entered his dwelling.

367. Gotama Buddha spread his double robe. He then laid down on it to sleep, like a brave lion in a rocky cave, free from fear and terror.

368. At that place, Soṇa Kuṭikaṇṇa, the disciple of the fully Enlightened Buddha who has sweet speech, recited the Dhamma in front of the best teacher, the Buddha.

369. This monk understood the reality of the Five Aggregates of clinging. He developed the Noble Eightfold Path and attained the highest peace. Now he can attain final extinguishing at passing away with a taint-free mind.

These verses were said by Arahant Soṇa Kuṭikaṇṇa.

The Verses of Arahant Kosiya

370. Truly, one should know the good Dhamma teacher's instructions. That wise person is obedient to the teacher's words. He has love and affection towards his teachers. He is indeed devoted and clever. He is an advanced person who has understood the Dhamma.

371. Without getting disturbed by any type of problem, he endures them patiently. He indeed is very strong and clever. He is an advanced person who has understood the Dhamma.

372. Freed from defilements, he is like a great ocean. He has profound wisdom. He can even understand very subtle meanings. Defilements can't challenge his purity. He is wise. He is an advanced person who has understood the Dhamma.

373. He has listened to a great deal of Dhamma. He has retained the Dhamma in his mind. He practices the Dhamma in accordance with the teaching. He is indeed equal to teachers. He is wise. He is an advanced person who has understood the Dhamma.

374. He understands the meaning of the Dhamma. Having understood, he acts accordingly. Truly he has attained the goal. He is wise. He is an advanced person who has understood the Dhamma.

These verses were said by Arahant Kosiya.

Section of Six Verses

The Verses of Arahant Uruveḷa Kassapa

375. The fame of Gotama Buddha was spreading everywhere. I saw his miracles. But because of my envy and pride, I did not bow down to worship him.

376. Superb trainer of beings, the Buddha knew my thoughts and reproached me. At that time, I felt very ashamed. Strange hair-raising excitement arose in me, making my body shiver.

377. It is true that in the past, when I was an ascetic with matted hair, I had a few supernormal powers. But I abandoned all of them. I became a monk in the Buddha's path.

378. Previously, I was satisfied with making sacrifices and intoxicated with enjoyments in the sensual realm. I abandoned all of them. Afterwards, I rooted out lust, hatred, and delusion too.

379. I gained the knowledge to understand my previous births. My divine eye is purified. I gained supernormal powers. I have the knowledge to read others' minds. I developed the divine ear.

380. I became a monk abandoning the home life to achieve a specific goal. I have achieved that goal and I have destroyed all fetters.

These verses were said by Arahant Uruveḷa Kassapa.

The Verses of Arahant Tekicchakāni

381. [Māra:] The rice is harvested and the store is full. But I don't get any alms. How shall I farm?

382. [Tekicchakāni:] With a confident mind, recollect the Supreme Buddha who has immeasurable qualities. Always live with a body that is filled and spread with joy and rapture.

383. With a confident mind, recollect the Supreme Dhamma that has immeasurable qualities. Always live with a body that is filled and spread with joy and rapture.

384. With a confident mind, recollect the Supreme Saṅgha that has immeasurable qualities. Always live with a body that is filled and spread with joy and rapture.

385. [Māra:] This is a cold winter night. You are outside. Do not perish disturbed by the cold. Go into a hut with all the windows and doors closed.

386. [Tekicchakāni:] I radiate thoughts of the Four Divine Abidings. I live experiencing happiness born of that meditation. I shall not perish because of the cold. I live without defilements.

These verses were said by Arahant Tekicchakāni.

The Verses of Arahant Mahānāga

387. If a monk doesn't have respect towards his fellow monks, he will decline in the Dhamma, like a fish in shallow water.

388. If a monk doesn't have respect towards his fellow monks, he will not grow in the Dhamma, like a rotten seed in a field.

389. If a monk doesn't have respect towards his fellow monks, he will go far away from Nibbāna in the path of the King of the Dhamma, the Buddha.

390. If a monk has respect towards his fellow monks, he will succeed in the Dhamma, like a fish swimming happily in a large lake.

391. If a monk has respect towards his fellow monks, he will grow in the Dhamma, like a good seed in a field.

392. If a monk has respect towards his fellow monks, he is very close to Nibbāna in the path of the King of the Dhamma, the Buddha.

These verses were said by Arahant Mahānāga.

The Verses of Arahant Kulla

393. My name is Kulla. One day I went to the cemetery. I saw a woman's dead body, thrown away, and full of worms. They were devouring it.

394. Kulla, see carefully this nasty body that is diseased, impure and rotten. Filth is oozing from the entire body. See this body that the fools delight in.

395. Taking the mirror of the Dhamma for the attainment of true knowledge and insight I investigated the true nature of the internal and external nasty body.

396. Both my body and the dead body are the same. What is in the dead body is in this body. Both the upper part and the lower part of the body just contain filth. Both parts are the same.

397. Filth oozes out from bodies in the day. Filth oozes out from bodies in the night. Both at night and day only filth oozes from bodies. Earlier, filth oozed out of bodies, and also later. Later and earlier only filth oozes from bodies.

398. In this way, with a one pointed mind. I contemplated the reality properly. At that time my mind delighted in the Dhamma. Not even the most pleasant fivefold music would give you that kind of happiness.

These verses were said by Arahant Kulla.

The Verses of Arahant Mālunkyaputta

399. If one is heedless in practicing the Dhamma, one's craving grows rapidly like a māluvā creeper that spirals around a big tree. He is like a monkey: desiring fruit, a monkey jumps from one tree to another. In the same way, this person journeys from one existence to another.

400. The evil craving that has invaded the whole world can overcome anybody. Then their grief grows like a bīrana grass shrub.

401. But, if one can overcome this evil craving that is hard to overcome, one's grief falls like a drop of water from a lotus leaf.

402. Now you have all gathered here. I will tell you a very good thing. The one who seeks the roots of bīrana grass uproots the bīrana shrub along with its roots. In just that same way, uproot craving with its roots. Just as a fast stream carries a bamboo twig, may Māra not destroy you again and again.

403. Do the word of the Buddha. Don't miss this precious moment. Those who miss this opportunity suffer, falling into hell.

404. Indeed, being heedless in practicing the Dhamma is a defilement in one's life. A defiled life is created from heedlessness. Therefore by heedfulness and true knowledge, one should pluck out one's own dart of craving.

These verses were said by Arahant Māluṅkyaputta.

The Verses of Arahant Sappadāsa

405. Twenty five years passed by since I became a monk. For this whole time, I could not obtain stillness of the mind, even for the time of a finger snap.

406. Having not obtained one-pointedness of mind at all, I suffered a lot from lust for sensual pleasures. Finally, weeping with my hands on my head I left the monastery.

407. I shall commit suicide with a knife. What is the meaning of this life? Having become a monk out of faith, how could I die as a layman, rejecting this holy life?

408. Then I took a razor and sat on my bed. I placed the razor on my throat thinking about cutting my vein.

409. Based on this incident, wise consideration arose in me. The danger of sensual pleasures was clear to me. Disenchantment with life was established in my mind.

410. Based on this same incident, my mind was liberated from all defilements. See the excellence of this Dhamma! I too attained the Triple Knowledge. The Buddha's path has been fully followed by me.

These verses were said by Arahant Sappadāsa.

The Verses of Arahant Kātiyāna

411. Hey Katiyana! Wake up now! Sit for meditation. Don't sleep like that! Be a good meditator, a wakeful meditator. May Māra, the relative of lazy people not trick and defeat you.

412. Birth and old age overwhelm you like waves of the great ocean. Make a safe island for yourself. There is no other external refuge for you.

413. Even your great teacher went beyond attachments and defeated the fear of birth and old age by practicing the Noble Eightfold Path. You should meditate day and night diligently. Practice the Dhamma very hard.

414. First, escape from the bondage of sensual pleasures. Wearing a double robe, shaving your hair with a razor, go on your alms round. Eat whatever you receive. Sleeping is called a sport. Don't delight in it. Dear Kātiyāna, meditate and follow the path.

415. Dear Kātiyāna, practice Jhānas. Win the battle over defilements. Be skilled in the path to Nibbāna. Obtain the unsurpassed purity. Attain final extinguishing at passing away, like a flame put out with water.

416. The ray of the lamp shines dimly. The flame leans back and forth gently in the wind and is fading away slowly. In the same way, don't cling to anything. Defeat Māra. Yes, now that monk got rid of desire for all feelings. He awaits the time to become cool and to attain final extinguishing at passing away.

These verses were said by Arahant Kātiyāna.

The Verses of Arahant Migajāla

417. The one with the eyes of Dhamma, the Buddha who was born in the clan of the sun, teaches Dhamma which overcomes all fetters and destroys all defilements.

418. This Dhamma path leads to Nibbāna; it makes people cross over saṁsāra; it dries up the roots of craving; it cuts off the vengeance, and brings people to Nibbāna.

419. This Dhamma path breaks the root of ignorance. It breaks the engine of kamma. Using knowledge as the diamond weapon, it hits wherever consciousness lands.

420. This Dhamma path shows you the true meaning of our feelings. It frees beings from grasping. Generating true knowledge, it shows the true nature of existence to be like a charcoal pit.

421. This Dhamma path prevents old age and death. It ends suffering. It releases the flavour of truth. That profound Dhamma path is the Noble Eightfold Path.

422. This Dhamma path enables people to understand kamma as kamma and result as result. It shows the reality of life through the mechanism of Dependant Origination. This soothing Dhamma path leading to a safe and peaceful state, is truly blissful until the end.

These verses were said by Arahant Migajāla.

The Verses of Arahant Jenta

423. I was intoxicated by my high-class birth, wealth, and status. I was also intoxicated by the beauty of my body.

424. I didn't care about anyone who was equal to me or elder to me. I was too stubborn. I was foolish to be so arrogant. I lived lifting high the flag of conceit.

425. I did not venerate anyone, neither mother nor father and no others regarded as honourable. That's how strong my stubbornness and disrespectfulness were.

426. But one day, I happened to see the supreme trainer of people to be tamed, the best teacher for the three worlds, the Buddha. I was looking at the great teacher who was walking like a blazing sun surrounded by many other monks.

427. My mind was pleased with that sight. I threw away all pride and intoxication. I knelt down with my head near the sacred feet of the best of all beings, the Buddha. I worshiped the Blessed One.

428. My pride of superiority and inferiority were eliminated and completely uprooted. The conceit "I" is cut out. All forms of conceit were destroyed.

These verses were said by Arahant Jenta.

The Verses of Arahant Sumana

429. I was newly ordained as a monk, and I was only seven years old. One day, I tamed a very vicious king snake, that had great supernormal powers, using my own supernormal powers.

430. That day I was bringing water from the great lake Anotatta for my preceptor. The great teacher saw me. Pointing me out, the great teacher, the Buddha said this:

431. Sāriputta, look at that young monk bringing a water pot. He is perfectly stilled inwardly.

432. His behavior is pleasing to others. Even the sight of him is wonderful for us. That novice monk is skilled in supernormal powers. He is excellent in the Dhamma. He is a pupil of Anuruddha.

433. He was made a great person by a great person. He was made a noble person by a noble person. He was trained and disciplined by Anuruddha who has already completed the path.

434. That novice Sumana has attained the highest peace. He is an enlightened one. But he doesn't want others to know that he is.

These verses were said by Arahant Sumana.

The Verses of Arahant Nahātakamuni

435. [The Blessed One:] Monk, you live in the great forest. You're suffering from an illness due to a wind disorder. You don't even receive enough of the four requisites. How do you live this tough life?

436. [Nahātakamuni:] Joy and happiness have spread through my body. It is because of this that I endure my tough life and live in the forest.

437. Developing the Seven Enlightenment Factors, Five Spiritual Faculties, Five Spiritual Powers and the subtle Jhānas, I live in this forest without taints.

438. I live free from defilements. My mind is not disturbed by anything. It is purified. I always investigate wisely. I live without taints.

439. Those internal and external taints I had previously were uprooted with nothing remaining. They will never rise again.

440. I fully understood the Five Aggregates of Clinging. Now they stand without roots. I achieved the destruction of suffering. There is no more rebirth for me.

These verses were said by Arahant Nahātakamuni.

The Verses of Arahant Brahmadatta

441. If someone is already tamed, leads a blameless life, freed from defilements with true understanding, calmed, has an unshaken mind, and is devoid of anger, how does anger arise in him?

442. The person who gets angry at another angry person loses his own wellbeing. But the person who does not get angry at another angry person wins the battle of defilements that is hard to win.

443. Knowing the other person is angry, if one is mindfully patient, he is the one who acts for the benefit of both parties of himself and of the other.

444. There are some foolish people who don't understand the value of this great Dhamma. They consider the person who acts for the benefit of both parties without getting angry to be a fool.

445. Therefore, if anger should arise in you, you should reflect upon the simile of the saw preached by the Buddha. (That is, you should not get angry even if someone cuts your limbs off with a saw.) If craving for tastes should arise in you, remember the simile of the child's flesh. (That is, think about how the parents crossing the desert felt when, after their only child died, they decided to eat his flesh in order to pass through the desert alive.)

446. If your mind runs among sensual pleasures and existences, quickly restrain it with mindfulness, as one restrains a bad cow from eating corn in a field.

These verses were said by Arahant Brahmadatta.

The Verses of Arahant Sirimaṇḍa

447. When the fault is covered, the defilements overflow. When the fault is disclosed, the defilements drain away. Therefore, one should be open without covering one's faults. As a result, defilements won't overflow and will drain away.

448. All beings in this world are attacked by death, surrounded by ageing. The dart of craving has been shot into them, and it smokes because of the things they desire.

449. All beings in this world are attacked by death and surrounded by ageing. They are beaten continuously, helplessly, like a thief who has received his punishment.

450. Death, diseases, and old age approach a person like huge fires from a volcano. There is no strength to fight against them, there is no speed to run away.

451. One should not make one's day unproductive, whether by a little or by much. Every night that is passed, his life span becomes shorter.

452. The last night can approach you at any time, whether you are walking, standing, sitting or lying down. Therefore, there is no time for you to be heedless.

These verses were said by Arahant Sirimaṇḍa.

The Verses of Arahant Sabbakāmi

453. One has to use this two legged, impure and evil smelling body. It is full of various types of filth. Only disgusting filth oozes from every door of this body.

454. But ordinary people are trapped in this body and suffer, like a deer stuck in a trap, a fish caught by the bait, or a monkey stuck to a sticky trap.

455. All the five cords of sensual pleasures—attractive sights, sounds, smells, tastes, and touch—are seen in the form of a woman.

456. With a lustful mind, ordinary people associate with a woman. The only thing they do is fill up the terrible cemetery in this long saṁsāra. They accumulate new kamma for future existences.

457. But if one avoids lust for women like one kicks away a snake's head, he overcomes craving for this life, established on clear mindfulness.

458. Understanding the dangers of sensual pleasures, seeing the giving up of sensual pleasures as a safe land, and abandoning all sensual pleasures, I became a monk. I attained enlightenment.

These verses were said by Arahant Sabbakāmi.

Section of Seven Verses

The Verses of Arahant Sundara Samudda

459. That woman was beautifully dressed, decorated with ornaments, wearing a flower garland. Her feet were coloured with red paint. She was wearing golden slippers. She was a prostitute.

460. She took off her slippers and stood before me, worshiping me with her joined palms. With a soft and sweet voice, this is what she said:

461. "Even though you were ordained, you are still very young. Listen to me. Enjoy human sensual pleasures. I will give you all comforts.

462. I promise you truly, I will even bring fire [by which to swear my commitment to you]. When we both reach old age, supported by walking sticks, let's go and ordain. This way we will win both worlds."

463. When I saw that prostitute, beautifully dressed and decorated with ornaments pleading with me, worshiping me with joined hands, it occurred to me that it was like a trap set by Māra.

464. Based on this incident, wise consideration arose in me. The danger of sensual pleasures was clear to me. Disenchantment with life was established in my mind.

465. Based on this same incident, my mind was liberated from all defilements. See the excellence of this Dhamma! I too attained the Triple Knowledge. The Buddha's path has been fully followed by me.

These verses were said by Arahant Sundara Samudda.

The Verses of Arahant Lakuṇṭaka Bhaddiya

466. That monk's name is Bhaddiya. He lives in a beautiful forest monastery called Ambāṭaka. Having uprooted craving, he meditates there happily.

467. To enjoy themselves, some people need drums, lutes, and cymbals. But I don't need any of those. I am sitting at the foot of this tree delighting in the path of the Buddha.

468. If the Supreme Buddha were to give me a boon and if I were to obtain that boon, I would take it on behalf of the whole world. That is, mindfulness in regard to the body that should be practiced at all times.

469. Some people make fun of me when looking at my physical appearance. But others get carried away by my sweet voice. Both groups are captured by desire and passion and they both don't know who I really am.

470. They don't see my internal life nor do they see my external life. Those foolish people are obstructed all around. They are just carried away only by my voice.

471. If one doesn't understand the internal life and sees only the external fruit, he will just be carried away by the external fruit, the voice.

472. But, if one understands both the internal and external lives, and sees the world fully opened, he will not be carried away by the voice.

These verses were said by Arahant Lakuṇṭaka Bhaddiya.

The Verses of Arahant Bhadda

473. I was the only child of the family. My mother and father loved me very much. To obtain a child, they performed many ceremonies with rituals and prayers. Then I was born.

474. Truly, my mother and father were very compassionate to me. Seeking my true happiness, they only wished for my wellbeing. One day, they carried me on their shoulders and took me to the Buddha, saying:

475. "Bhante, this son was obtained by great difficulty. He is very delicate and has only prospered in happiness. Great teacher, you are the protector of this world and the victor of great battles. Now we offer this child to you to train as your pupil."

476. The great teacher accepted me and said to Ānanda Bhante, "Ānanda, ordain this child quickly. This child will become outstanding."

477. Having ordained me, the Great Victor entered the monastery. Within a short time, before the sun could even set, my mind was liberated from all defilements.

478. That day, the Great Teacher, rising up from his meditation, called me thus, "Dear Bhadda, come here." That was my higher ordination.

479. I was just seven years old when I received higher ordination. I too attained the Triple Knowledge. Ah! See the excellence of this Dhamma.

These verses were said by Arahant Bhadda.

The Verses of Arahant Sopāka

480. The shadow of the Buddha's hut fell on his walking path. The best of men, the Buddha, was doing walking meditation there. I went up to him. I worshiped him, the best of men, the Buddha.

481. I arranged in my robe, putting it over one shoulder. Placing my hands together, I too started walking behind the Buddha, the one who is freed from defilements, the best of all beings.

482. The Buddha who is extremely skilled in answering questions asked me questions. At that time, I was not scared or terrified at all to answer. I answered all the questions.

483. The Tathāgata Buddha was pleased at the way I answered the questions. Looking at the community of monks, the Buddha said this about me:

484. "The people of Aṅga and Magadha offer robes, food, resting places and medicine to this young monk Sopāka. This young Sopāka uses them. It's a great gain for those people. Those people, having seen this young monk, get up from their seats and pay respect to him. It's a great gain for those people. Those people have Dhamma discussions with this young monk. It's a great gain for them.

485. Dear Sopāka, from today onwards you should come to see me. Dear Sopāka, just your answering of my questions is your higher ordination."

486. I was just seven years old when I received higher ordination. I too attained the Triple Knowledge. Ah! See the excellence of this Dhamma.

These verses were said by Arahant Sopāka.

The Verses of Arahant Sarabhaṅga

487. Previously, I used to break off reed grass with my hands and make my hut. Since I lived in that hut, I was called "Sarabhaṅga," reed breaker.

488. But now I am not allowed to break off reed grass with my hands. Our great teacher, the famous Gotama Buddha has laid down training rules for us.

489. I am Sarabhaṅga. But previously I did not see the entire disease of saṃsāra like this. Having followed the words of the Buddha, the great teacher higher than the devas, I have realized the entire disease of saṃsāra.

490. Whatever path traveled by Vipassi Buddha, Sikhī Buddha, Vessabhu Buddha, Kakusandha Buddha, Konāgamana Buddha, and Kassapa Buddha, our Gotama Buddha also traveled on that very same path.

491. These seven Supreme Buddhas have attained Nibbāna. These Buddhas are freed from craving and clinging. These Buddhas are born from the Dhamma. With unshakeable minds, these Buddhas taught this Dhamma.

492. Out of compassion for beings these Supreme Buddhas taught the Dhamma, the Four Noble Truths: suffering, the cause of suffering, the path leading to the cessation of suffering and the cessation, the destruction of suffering.

493. If the endless suffering of journeying on in saṁsāra comes to an end in one's life, when life is finished the body breaks up, there is no rebirth for that person. I too am such a person. I am liberated from defilements, saṁsāra; everything.

These verses were said by Arahant Sarabhaṅga.

Section of Eight Verses

The Verses of Arahant Mahā Kaccāyana

494. A monk should not always be occupied doing many duties. A monk should avoid people who gossip and talk unnecessarily. If a monk is greedy and desires nice things, he will miss the goal which brings spiritual happiness.

495. Indeed, wise people consider respect and homage given by others to be a swamp. Attachment to gain and honour is like a fine dart that is hard to remove. An untrue person will never give up gain and honour offered to him.

496. One should not insist others do evil nor should he do it himself. I say that because all beings live with kamma as their relative.

497. One is not a thief just because others say one is. One is not a holy man just because others say one is. One knows oneself to the extent that devas know who he is.

498. Foolish people don't understand that we all will die one day in this world. But since wise people understand this fact, their quarrels cease.

499. Even after the loss of his wealth, the wise man indeed lives. But no matter how much wealth one has, if he hasn't gained wisdom he is not truly living.

500. Even though a wise person hears all with the ear, sees all with the eye, he doesn't want to take it in nor reject that which is seen or heard.

501. Therefore, at things that shouldn't be seen, he is as though blind even though he has eyes. At the things that shouldn't be heard, he is as though deaf even though he has ears. At things

that shouldn't be known, he is as though foolish even though he is wise. At things that shouldn't be done, he is as though weak even though he is strong. At things that lead to harm he is as though dead, lying in bed.

These verses were said by Arahant Mahā Kaccāyana.

The Verses of Arahant Sirimitta

502. If a monk doesn't get angry and doesn't hate anyone, is not deceitful, and is devoid of divisive speech, truly he doesn't grieve after death.

503. If a monk doesn't get angry and doesn't hate anyone, is not deceitful, is devoid of divisive speech, and lives with sense doors guarded, truly he doesn't grieve after death.

504. If a monk doesn't get angry and doesn't hate anyone, is not deceitful, is devoid of divisive speech, and lives with good, virtuous behavior, truly he doesn't grieve after death.

505. If a monk doesn't get angry and doesn't hate anyone, is not deceitful, is devoid of divisive speech, and lives with noble friends, truly he doesn't grieve after death.

506. If a monk doesn't get angry and doesn't hate anyone, is not deceitful, is devoid of divisive speech, and lives with good wisdom, truly he doesn't grieve after death.

507–8. If one has an unshakable and well-established confidence in the Tathāgata, the Buddha, and has good virtue pleasing to and praised by the noble ones, if one has a pleasant mind towards the community of monks, and has a straight view, the Buddhas look at him as not poor. His life is not in vain.

509. Therefore a wise person remembering the Buddha's teaching, establishing confidence in the Buddha, practicing virtue,

having a pleasant mind and developing a clear understanding of the Dhamma, should practice the Supreme Dhamma.

These verses were said by Arahant Sirimitta.

The Verses of Arahant Mahāpanthaka

510. When I first saw the Great Teacher who lives without any fear at all, that moment, seeing the Best of Men, a sense of shame about myself arose in me.

511. The one who doesn't accept the advice of the Great Teacher, the Buddha, is like the one who hits with his hands and feet the goddess of fortune who comes to his house and tells her to get out.

512. Considering this, I abandoned my wife and children, money and properties. Having shaven my head and beard, I became a monk in the Buddha's path.

513. Protecting precepts, following right livelihood, guarding my sense doors and worshiping the Supreme Buddha, I live unbeatable.

514. Those days, just one wish was firmly established in my heart: Until I remove this dart of craving from my life I will not sit down even for a moment.

515. I lived with such energy. See my strong effort. I achieved the Triple Knowledge. The Buddha's path has been fully followed by me.

516. I gained the knowledge to see my previous births. My divine eye is purified. I became an enlightened one. Now I am worthy of offerings. I am completely liberated from defilements.

517. As soon as the sun rose ending the night, having dried up all craving, I sat cross legged.

These verses were said by Arahant Mahāpanthaka.

Section of Nine Verses

The Verses of Arahant Bhūta

518. Ordinary people are enveloped in ignorance. As a result they live attached to suffering followed by ageing and death. The wise monk knows about this. So that monk can understand that suffering completely. He can meditate very mindfully. He is delighted and finds nothing happier than this meditation bliss.

519. This craving drags beings only towards suffering. Having been tied up with defilements, craving brings only pain. That monk could strike down that craving. He could meditate very mindfully. He doesn't have anything happier than this.

520. The best of paths, the Noble Eight Fold Path, which cleanses all defilements, is a wonderful path. That monk saw that blissful path with wisdom. He meditates very mindfully. He doesn't have anything happier than this.

521. There is no sorrow or stain in the unconditioned, peaceful Nibbāna. He attained that Nibbāna which cleanses all defilements and cuts all fetters and attachments. He doesn't have anything happier than this.

522. The sky is thundering. The whole sky is covered with rain. That monk meditates in a mountain cave. He doesn't have anything happier than this.

523. Wild flowers are very beautiful. When the wind blows, the falling petals spread all around the banks of the river. That monk meditates sitting on the bank of that river. He doesn't have anything happier than this.

524. At night it rains in the thick forest. At that time, elephants trumpet and cry. That monk meditates in a mountain cave. He doesn't have anything happier than this.

525. That monk has abandoned all unwholesome thoughts. He lives without distress and the thorns of defilements. He meditates in a cleft among mountains. He doesn't have anything happier than this.

526. Having destroyed stains of ignorance, thorns of sorrow, distress, dart of craving, and thorns of defilements, he eradicated all taints. With a peaceful mind, that monk meditates. He doesn't have anything happier than this.

These verses were said by Arahant Bhūta.

The Verses of Arahant Kāḷudāyi

527. Great sage, the trees have dropped their leaves and time has come for fruit to grow. The blossoming flowers glow like burning coal. Those trees shine like flames. Great hero, time has come to help your relatives, the Sākyans.

528. Those delightful trees in bloom spread their sweet scent all around. Now those trees dropped their leaves and are hoping to bear fruit. Great hero, time has come for us to leave from here.

529. Great sage, it is not too cold or too hot. The season is pleasant for a long journey. When the Blessed One walks crossing the Rohini river, may the Sākyans and Koliyans from the west have a chance to see you, the Blessed One.

530. Farmers plow a paddy field out of desire. They scatter seeds desirously. Merchants travel across the ocean to find money desirously. I too have a desire. May my desire be fulfilled.

531. Again and again farmers scatter seeds. Again and again it rains. Again and again farmers plow paddy fields. Again and again grain comes to the kingdom.

532. Again and again beggars ask for things. Again and again givers give things. Again and again givers, having given things, again and again are reborn in heaven.

533. If a great hero of great wisdom is born into a certain family, indeed that person's birth is for the wellbeing of seven generations. I think that, like the greatest god among gods, the Blessed One can give far more relief to the world. You, the Blessed One, are the only one who can be called "the truth."

534. The father of the Great Seer is king Suddhodana. The queen, bearing the Bodhisatta baby in her womb, took care of the baby. After death, she was reborn in Tusita heaven and delighted there. The mother of the Buddha is Māyā.

535. The Buddha's mother, having passed away from this world, met with divine pleasures. Surrounded by many goddesses, she enjoys divine sensual pleasures there.

536. The Buddha is unique and unconquered. The Buddha has an unshaken mind. I am a son of the Buddha, oh Sākya King Suddhodana. Therefore you are my father's father. King from Gotama clan, by the Dhamma you are my grandfather.

These verses were said by Arahant Kāḷudāyi.

The Verses of Arahant Eka Vihāriya

537. When I am alone in the forest, if no one else is behind or in front of me, truly I feel at ease.

538. The Buddha highly praised living in the forest. Yes, I too shall go to the forest alone. For a monk who practices the Dhamma giving it top priority, living alone is pleasing.

539. I'm a meditator. I really like to enter the forest where elephants and tuskers live. The forest is delightful. Alone I enter the forest immediately with big hope.

540. The field is filled with blooming flowers. The forest is cool. I wash myself and start doing walking meditation alone.

541. When shall I live truly alone, companionless in this beautiful great forest as an enlightened one who has done what had to be done to end suffering?

542. That is how I wish to be. May my wish come true. I should proceed on the path by myself. No one can follow the path for another.

543. I go to the forest wearing my brave armour. I shall not come out of the forest until I have eliminated all the taints.

544. The cool wind blows giving a sweet smell, just like a divine fragrance. Sitting on the top of the mountain, I shall split ignorance.

545. The forest is filled with fragrant flowers. I live in cool caves in the mountain joyfully, delighting in the happiness of liberation.

546. Everything I wished for has now been fulfilled. My life is like the full moon in the sky. I eliminated all the taints. There is no more rebirth for me.

These verses were said by Arahant Eka Vihāriya.

The Verses of Arahant Mahā Kappina

547. Planning in advance for a good future, if one acts understanding what is beneficial and unbeneficial, he is very wise. Neither enemies nor friends will see a weak spot in him.

548. One should practice mindfulness of breathing exactly as taught by the Buddha. If one completes and develops mindfulness very well like that, he can illuminate this world, like the moon freed from clouds.

549. Truly, my mind is now well purified. Since it has been well developed without limit, putting forth energy wisely, the mind illuminates all the directions.

550. Even after the loss of his wealth, the wise person lives. But, if one doesn't have wisdom, no matter how rich he is, he doesn't live.

551. Once wisdom is the key factor, it connects the Dhamma one has heard to one's life. The same wisdom generates fame and good reputation for that person. In this world, the person with wisdom finds happiness even in painful situations.

552. The following truth is not only relevant to today. This is not even amazing or strange. If someone is born, that person dies. What indeed is strange in that?

553. At the very same moment one is born, that birth is tied to death. As long as one is born, one has to die. That is the nature of all beings.

554. When someone cries over a dead body, it doesn't do that dead one any good. Fame and praise cannot be gained by weeping over a dead body in this world. Such weeping is not praised by recluses and brāhmins.

555. Weeping impairs the eyes and the body. The good appearance of the body fades away. Mindfulness and awareness get weakened. The weeper's enemies become joyful. His relatives and friends become unhappy.

556. Therefore, those householders should desire to associate with wise noble ones who are well versed in the Dhamma. Those noble ones act through great wisdom. Their lives are like a ship crossing to the far shore of a great river.

These verses were said by Arahant Mahā Kappina.

The Verses of Arahant Cūḷapanthaka

557. Previously, I was very weak in understanding the Dhamma. Those days, I was greatly despised. Even my own brother excluded me from the monastery, saying "Now you should leave and go home!"

558. Being excluded by my own brother, I was standing sadly at the gateway of the monastery. Still, I loved the path of the Buddha.

559. The Blessed One came there. My great teacher stroked my head. Taking me by the hand, the Blessed One led me into the monastery again.

560. Indeed the great teacher was compassionate towards me. The teacher gave me a piece of foot wiping cloth and instructed me to go off and focus my mindfulness well on that piece of white cloth.

561. I took my great teacher's words into my heart. I practiced the Buddha's path delightfully. I developed that one-pointedness which directly led me to the supreme goal, Nibbāna.

562. Now I have the knowledge to recollect my previous lives. I also purified my divine eye. I have achieved the Triple Knowledge. The Buddha's path has been fully followed by me.

563. That day, I, monk Panthaka, created thousands of monks that looked just like me. I was sitting in that beautiful mango grove until the time for the meal was announced.

564. Then, my great teacher sent a messenger to me to announce the time for the meal. That day, I went to the meal through the sky.

565. I worshiped my Great Teacher's sacred feet and sat down to one side. My great teacher only accepted food once he saw that I was seated.

566. The one who is worthy of the offering of the whole world, the field of merit of humans, the Buddha, accepted the meal.

These verses were said by Arahant Cūḷapanthaka.

The Verses of Arahant Kappa

567–68. Like a sewer full of filth, like a disgusting pool of dung, like a nasty wound, like a boil full of puss, born in a womb, full of puss and blood, heavy with excrement and urine, trickling filth all the time, disgusting things always ooze out of the body.

569. Having a binding of sixty tendons, plastered with flesh, wrapped with a dress called skin, this foul body is worthless.

570. Linked together with a skeleton of bones, with bonds of sinew threads, the body produces its various postures by the union of many filthy things.

571. Definitely heading toward death, this body is always close to death. Having abandoned this body here, finally the person goes somewhere else.

572. The true nature of this body is covered with ignorance. Tied with knots of defilements, this body is sinking down in the flood of defilements. It is caught in the net of hidden defilements.

573. Joined with the five hindrances, surrounded by lavish thoughts, rooted by craving, this house called "body" is roofed with rafters of delusion.

574. With such a nature, this body functions by the engine called kamma. Life ends whether you have gain or loss. Changing is the only nature of life.

575. If somebody regards such a body to be their own, they are blind, ordinary people. They just fill up this fearful saṁsāra. Repeated journeying in saṁsāra continues for them.

576. Therefore, if somebody avoids this body like avoiding a snake smeared in dung, having uprooted existence with its root, he will attain final extinguishing at passing away without taints.

These verses were said by Arahant Kappa.

The Verses of Arahant Upasena

577. A monk should live in a place suitable for meditation. Far away, quiet, and secluded forests inhabited by wild animals are ideal places.

578. A monk should wear the coarse robe which was sewn from rags, taken from a heap of rubbish, a cemetery or the streets.

579. A monk should walk for alms from house to house without exception, making his mind humble. He should walk with his sense doors guarded and well restrained.

580. He should be content, even with coarse food. He should not seek many various flavours. The mind of one who is greedy for flavours does not delight in meditation.

581. One should live desiring very little and content with whatever is available. Without mingling in the company of lay people and monastics, a sage should live alone.

582. A wise monk stays in the midst of the monks as if he knows nothing and has no voice. He should not speak excessively.

583. A monk should not insult anyone. He should not hurt anyone. He should be restrained by the rules of discipline and should know the purpose of eating.

584. A monk should be skilled in handling the meditation object which gives rise to energy of mind. He should practice serene and insight meditations at the right time.

585. A monk should meditate always putting forth energy and effort. A wise monk doesn't give up hope until he has achieved Nibbāna, putting an end to all suffering.

586. When a monk lives in this way, desiring noble purity, all his taints are eradicated, and he attains extinguishing.

These verses were said by Arahant Upasena.

The Verses of Arahant Apara Gotama

587. The one who wishes for his own good should find out about the teaching of the Buddha. He should also find out about the practice fitting for recluses.

588. Association with noble friends, training in higher virtue, and a desire to listen to the teachers' advice—these good qualities are very fitting for a recluse's life.

589. Respect towards the Buddha, loyalty towards the Dhamma, hospitality towards the community of monks—these good qualities are very fitting for a recluse's life.

590. Well-disciplined behaviour, a pure and blameless life, and settling the mind in meditation—these good qualities are very fitting for a recluse's life.

591. Knowing proper manners, acting with pleasant postures, and practicing serene and insight meditations, these good qualities are very fitting for a recluse's life.

592. Living in secluded, faraway, quiet forest monasteries where sages dwell is very fitting for a recluse's life.

593. Being virtuous, having vast learning of the Dhamma, investigating the true nature of life and realizing the Four Noble Truths, these good qualities are very fitting for a recluse's life.

594. Developing the perception of impermanence, perception of non-self, perception of unattractiveness, and distaste towards the whole world as meditations: these good qualities are very fitting for a recluse's life.

595. Developing the enlightenment factors, the bases for supernormal powers, the five spiritual faculties, the five spiritual pow-

ers and the Noble Eightfold Path: these good qualities are very fitting for a recluse's life.

596. The sage abandons craving, uproots the taints with their roots, and lives liberated from everything: these good qualities are very fitting for recluse's life.

These verses were said by Arahant Apara Gotama.

Section of Eleven Verses

The Verses of Arahant Saṅkicca

597. Dear monk, what are you looking for, staying in this thick forest in the mountain Ujjuhana in this rainy season? Do you really like this chilly wind? Meditators like to live alone.

598. In the rainy season, strong winds carry clouds through the sky. In the same way, thoughts connected to seclusion overwhelm my mind.

599. All the time there are crows covering the cemetery. When I see those birds, mindfulness connected to thoughts of dispassion about this body arises in me.

600. If others do not protect him, and if he does not protect others, that kind of monk sleeps happily having no hopes for sensual pleasures.

601. The stream with clear water and a rocky slope is very beautiful. Monkeys and other animals have lots of fun there. Those mountains covered with moss delight my heart.

602. I have lived in forests, beside water falls, in caves, and in faraway monasteries inhabited by beasts.

603. I am not aware of having any evil and angry thoughts such as, "May these beings be killed, may they be slaughtered and may they come to harm."

604. The Great Teacher's instruction has been respectfully followed by me. The Buddha's path has been fully followed by me. I lowered the heavy load of defilements. I rooted out the fetters of existence.

605. I became a monk with the wish to achieve one goal – the destruction of all fetters. That, I have achieved.

606. I don't desire to die nor do I desire to live. Like a person who is awaiting his monthly salary, I am awaiting my time to attain final extinguishing at passing away.

607. I don't long for death, I don't long for life, with clear mindfulness and awareness I am awaiting the day to attain final extinguishing at passing away.

These verses were said by Arahant Saṅkicca.

Section of Twelve Verses

The Verses of Arahant Sīlava

608. One should diligently practice virtue in this Buddha's path. Here in this world, well practiced virtue brings all success.

609. A wise person should practice virtue desiring three types of happiness: praise, the gaining of wealth, and rejoicing in heaven after death.

610. By his restrained life, a virtuous person acquires many friends. But the unvirtuous person is separated from his friends because of his evil actions.

611. The unvirtuous person only gains a bad reputation and blame. The virtuous person always gains a good reputation, fame and praise.

612. Virtue is the foundation and base for wholesome qualities. Virtue is like a mother for all good qualities. Virtue is the foremost of all good qualities. Therefore, one should make one's virtue pure.

613. The mind is like the great ocean. Virtue is like its beach. Virtue, the dock of merit of all Buddhas, gives joy and restraint. Therefore, one should make one's virtue pure.

614. Virtue is an incomparable power. Virtue is the supreme weapon. Virtue is the best ornament. Virtue is a marvelous armour.

615. Virtue is a very mighty bridge. Virtue is an unsurpassed perfume. Virtue is the best scent which spreads in all directions.

616. Virtue is the supreme food for the journey. Virtue is the foremost source of wealth for a journey. Virtue is the best vehicle in which one can travel in all directions.

617. An evil person gets blamed in this world and after death he has to suffer having being born in hell. That fool falls into suffering everywhere due to lack of virtue and an unstill mind.

618. A well behaved person obtains fame in this world and after death is happy in heaven. That wise, energetic person is happy everywhere due to his virtuous behavior and a perfectly still mind.

619. Virtue is great in this Dhamma path but wisdom is the greatest. One can achieve victory among humans and gods through one's virtue and wisdom.

These verses were said by Arahant Sīlava.

The Verses of Arahant Sunīta

620. I was born in a low-class family, poor, having little food. My job was very lowly: I was a disposer of people's feces.

621. People shunned me, disgraced me and insulted me. So, making my mind humble, I paid homage to many people.

622. But I was extraordinarily fortunate. One day I saw the great hero, the Buddha, entering the famous city of Rājagaha, surrounded by a large community of monks.

623. I put down my rack of buckets of feces. I approached the Buddha to worship the sacred feet of the Blessed One. At that time, out of sympathy for me, the best of beings, the Supreme Buddha, stood still.

624. I worshiped my great teacher's sacred feet. Then I stood up to one side. I begged to become a monk, the best life of all.

625. Then the merciful great teacher, compassionate towards the whole world, said to me, "Come, monk." That was my higher ordination.

626. I live in the forest alone. I'm not lazy. I fully followed the instruction exactly as the Buddha advised me.

627. In the first watch of the night, I gained the knowledge to recollect my previous lives. In the middle watch of the night, I purified my divine eye. In the last watch of the night, I tore apart the thick darkness of ignorance.

628. Then at the end of the night, towards sunrise, the God Sakka and the Great Brahma came and worshiped me with hands together.

629. "Homage to you, thoroughbred of men! Homage to you, best of men! Great sage, your mind is fully freed from all taints. You are worthy of the offerings of the world."

630. My great teacher saw the assembly of gods surrounding me and smiled. Then the great teacher said this:

631. "By austerity, by living the holy life, by self-restraint and self-taming, one becomes a Brāhmin. Here there is a Supreme Brāhmin."

These verses were said by Arahant Sunīta.

Section of Thirteen Verses

The Verses of Arahant Soṇa

632. He was a member of the ruling government who worked for the king of Aṅga. Those days he was very powerful. His name is Soṇa. Today he is also very powerful, but in the Dhamma. He has crossed over all suffering.

633. One should cut off five [lower fetters]. One should abandon five [higher fetters]. One should especially develop five [spiritual faculties]. One should go beyond the five knots of [lust, hatred, delusion, conceit, and views]. That monk is called the "flood-crosser."

634. If a monk has a lot of pride in himself, if he is heedless and if he desires external things, he won't be able to fulfill the training of virtue, one-pointedness of mind and wisdom.

635. The one who has a lot of pride in himself and is heedless abandons what should be done and does what should not be done. The result will be the increase of the taints.

636. But if one constantly practices mindfulness with regard to the body he will not do what shouldn't be done, but will continuously do what should be done. Due to his clear mindfulness and wise awareness, his taints come to an end.

637. The Noble Eightfold Path is the only straight way pointed out by the Great Teacher. Follow that way only. Do not turn back. Judge your own mistakes and reprimand yourself. That person will achieve Nibbāna.

638. I put too much effort in practicing the Dhamma. The great teacher, unsurpassed in the world, the one with eyes of Dhamma, taught me the Dhamma using the simile of the guitar.

639. I accepted the Great Teacher's words respectfully. I started the practice again delighting in the Buddha's path. I also developed serene meditation heading to Nibbāna. I achieved the Triple Knowledge. The Buddha's path has been fully followed by me.

640–41. Having dropped the whole world from the mind, having made the mind secluded and free from sorrow, I eradicated desire for the Five Aggregates of Clinging, and dedicated myself to abandon craving. Without being deluded by anything, when I saw the true nature of the sense bases, my mind was fully liberated from all defilements.

642. When the mind is fully liberated from defilements it is very calm. There is nothing to add to the completed path. Nothing remains to be done.

643. Just as a huge solid rock is not moved by the wind, so too sights, sounds, smells, tastes and touches—

644. None of these pleasant or unpleasant things can agitate that monk. That monk has an untroubled mind. His mind is established in Nibbāna. It doesn't mix with anything else. That monk can see very clearly how everything is changing.

These verses were said by Arahant Soṇa.

Section of Fourteen Verses

The Verses of Arahant Khadiravaniya Revata

645. From the day I became a monk, abandoning the home life, until now I don't recall having any thoughts of hatred in my mind.

646. For this long period of time I have not been aware of having even a slight intention such as, "may these beings be killed, may they be slaughtered, may they come to harm."

647. I have been fully aware of practicing loving-kindness meditation very well, immeasurably, gradually and exactly as taught by the Supreme Buddha.

648. I develop a mind of loving kindness toward friends, acquaintances and all beings, always delighting in non-harming.

649. Truly, rapture is generated by immoveable and unshakeable-loving kindness. Foolish people don't practice this. But I practice all four divine abiding meditations.

650. The monk, the disciple of the Supreme Buddha, calls that Jhāna which is devoid of thoughts noble silence. That monk attains that Jhāna.

651. Just as a rocky mountain is unmoveable and firm, the monk who eradicated delusion is like a mountain. He does not tremble.

652. To a person who lives without evil and always seeks purity, a hair's tip measure of fault seems as if it is the size of a big cloud.

653. Just as a city is well guarded inside and out, so you should guard yourselves without letting your life follow the wrong way. Don't miss this great opportunity.

654. I don't desire death nor do I desire to live. Like a person who is waiting for his monthly salary, I am awaiting my time to attain final extinguishing at passing away.

655. I don't desire death, I don't desire life, with clear mindfulness and wise awareness I am awaiting the day to attain final extinguishing at passing away.

656. The Great Teacher's instruction has been respectfully followed by me. The Buddha's path has been fully followed by me. I lowered the heavy load of defilements. I rooted out the fetters of existence.

657. I became a monk with the wish to achieve one goal. That, I have achieved. I have cut all fetters.

658. Therefore, dear people, this is my only advice to you: practice the path to Nibbāna diligently. I will absolutely attain final extinguishing at passing away. I am liberated from all suffering.

These verses were said by Arahant Khadiravaniya Revata.

The Verses of Arahant Godatta

659. A noble thoroughbred ox when tied to its cart drags the heavy load easily undisturbed by the weight. It doesn't try to avoid its duty.

660. The wise monk is exactly like that. He is like a great ocean filled with water. He is fully satisfied with his wisdom. He does not despise others. This is a great quality of such noble ones.

661. Beings suffer because they are carried away by time and by being stuck in time. They suffer because they are carried away by existence and by being stuck in existence. Therefore they grieve right here in this world.

662. When foolish people undergo happiness, they are overjoyed and intoxicated with pride. When they undergo pain they are deprived in sadness. Not understanding the true nature of this

life, those foolish people are depressed by both happiness and pain.

663. Craving sews existences together creating happiness and pain. Those who overcome this craving can live unshaken like a deeply planted stone pillar. They can live without being over-joyed or depressed.

664. No matter if they gain or lose something. No matter if they gain a bad reputation or a good reputation. No matter if they gain blame or praise. No matter if they gain happiness or unhappiness. They are not agitated.

665. They don't stick to any object just like a drop of water doesn't stick to a lotus leaf. Those wise, energetic people are happy every-where. They are unconquered everywhere.

666. If loss comes from a righteous life and profit comes from an unrighteous life, of these two, righteous loss is indeed better than an unrighteous profit.

667. If appreciation comes to somebody from foolish people and criticism comes from wise people, of these two, criticism from the wise is better than appreciation from fools.

668. If praise comes to somebody from foolish people and blame comes from wise people, of these two, the correction from the wise is indeed better than the praise from the fools.

669. Of happiness coming from sensual pleasures and pain com-ing from giving up sensual pleasures, truly pain coming from seclusion is better than the happiness that comes from sensual pleasures.

670. Of living an unrighteous life and death from righteous living, truly, righteous death is better than unrighteous living.

671. Those who have eliminated the desire for sensual pleasures and anger, those who are unattached to any existence, those

who live in the world without craving, for them there is nothing agreeable to get attached to or disagreeable to be rejected.

672. Having developed the enlightenment factors, spiritual faculties and spiritual powers, those enlightened ones attain the highest peace and attain final extinguishing at passing away.

These verses were said by Arahant Godatta.

Section of Sixteen Verses

The Verses of Arahant Aññākoṇḍañña

673. This Dhamma has a wonderful taste. When I heard that excellent Dhamma, I gained great confidence in it. This Dhamma taught by the Supreme Buddha is a passion-free teaching that leads to complete detachment.

674. There are various objects in this world. I think that the thoughts connected with these colorful objects arousing lust, stir up the whole world.

675. Just as dust blown by the wind settles when it rains, so lustful thoughts fade away when one understands them with wisdom.

676. With developed wisdom, when one contemplates all conditioned things as impermanent, he becomes disenchanted with suffering. This is the way to purification.

677. With developed wisdom, when one contemplates all conditioned things as suffering, he becomes disenchanted with suffering. This is the way to purification.

678. With developed wisdom, when one contemplates all phenomena as non-self, he becomes disenchanted with suffering. This is the way to purification.

679. This elder Koṇḍañña followed the Buddha very closely. This monk is strong in energy. That is why he could eliminate birth and death. He perfected living the holy life.

680. There is a huge flood. There are snares everywhere. There are strong spears and there is a mountain hard to split. This elder broke all the spears, destroyed all the snares and split into pieces the mountain that was hard to split. He crossed over the flood

and reached the far shore. He is a meditator. He is released from the bond of Māra.

681. If a monk is conceited, vain, and delights in the association of evil friends, he will sink down into the whirlpool called anger and drown in the great flood of saṁsāra.

682. The wise monk who is not conceited, not vain, and who acts prudently, restraining sense bases, and associating with noble friends, will put an end to suffering.

683. His hands and legs are very thin like the knots of the kāla plant. His veins are popping out. He knows very well the purpose of taking food. He has a strong, brave heart.

684. He goes to the thick forest to meditate. There, when he is attacked by mosquitos and harmful insects, he endures them with clear mindfulness, like a king elephant in the battlefield.

685. I don't desire death nor do I desire life. Like a person who is awaiting his monthly salary, I am awaiting my time to attain final Nibbāna at passing away.

686. I don't desire death nor do I desire life. With clear mindfulness and awareness, I am awaiting the day to attain final Nibbāna at passing away.

687. The Great Teacher's instruction has been respectfully followed by me. The Buddha's path has been fully followed by me. I lowered the heavy load of defilements. I rooted out the fetters of existence.

688. I became a monk with the wish to achieve one goal. That, I have achieved. So, what do I need anyone else for? (I am liberated from everything.)

These verses were said by Arahant Aññākoṇḍañña.

The Verses of Arahant Udāyi

689. This great being was born in the human world. This sage tamed himself, stilled the mind, made his conduct and behaviour pure, and lived delighting in the calming of the mind.

690. This great being, having reached the far shore, was released from everything in the world. Humans worship the Supreme Buddha. Gods also worship the Supreme Buddha; I heard this from the enlightened ones.

691. The Supreme Buddha, liberated from all fetters, came out of the forest of defilements. The Blessed One, giving up sensual pleasures, delighted in a secluded life. The Supreme Buddha is like a golden ornament that slides down smoothly from a rocky mountain top.

692. The Blessed One is indeed like the most beautiful elephant in the world. He is like the beautiful Himalaya Mountain which surpasses all the other mountains. The Blessed One is like a king elephant, extremely great and his name is indeed "Truth."

693. Now I am going to describe the excellent king elephant to you. This elephant does no sin whatsoever. His front feet are virtue and compassion.

694. The elephant's hind feet are clear mindfulness and wise awareness. This elephant has a beautiful trunk. Its name is faith. The elephant has two white tusks. Their names are equanimity.

695. This elephant's beautiful neck is truth. His large head is wisdom. He has Dhamma intentions with wise consideration. His belly is the true Dhamma. He has a tail called seclusion.

696. Internally he has a perfectly still mind. He delights in extinguishing. He meditates. This elephant walks and stands with a stilled mind.

697. This elephant sleeps and sits with a stilled mind. He is restrained all the time. This is his success.

698. This elephant eats only what is received righteously. He never eats things that are received unrighteously. When he is offered food, drink and robes, he never stores them up.

699. He has cut every fetter and bond, large or small. Wherever he goes, he goes without any expectation.

700. The white lotus that grows in water is very beautiful and sweet smelling. But its flower is not touching the water.

701. The Buddha, born in this world, is exactly the same. The Buddha lives in this world like a lotus that is not touching the water. His life is not touched by anything that defiles the ordinary world.

702. A great blazing fire is extinguished when it has run out of fuel, and when the fire is dead and ashes arise, it is called "extinguished."

703. This simile has been taught by the wise noble ones. Great enlightened ones are like great king elephants. I too am such an elephant. That is why I was able to recognize and describe the greatest king elephant called the Buddha.

704. This great king elephant called the Buddha doesn't have any desire, hatred, or delusion. He is freed from all taints. Therefore, when the Buddha abandons the body here, he will attain final extinguishing.

These verses were said by Arahant Udāyi.

Section of Twenty Verses

The Verses of Arahant Adhimutta

705. [Thieves:] In the past, we killed people for sacrifice or for wealth. When we caught them, they were very afraid, trembled with fear, and screamed.

706. But amazingly, you don't seem to be scared at all. Your body just shines more and more. Even in such a fearful situation, how are you not terrified?

707. [Arahant Adhimutta:] Dear leader of the thieves, I live without desires. I don't have any mental pain. Truly, everything that brings fear can be overcome by one who has eradicated all fetters.

708. When one understands the Four Noble Truths fully, all chains of existence break apart. When the burden of defilements is dropped, there is no fear at death.

709. This holy life has been well practiced by me. The way to extinguishing has been well completed. I have no fear at death. For me, death is like the curing of a disease.

710. This holy life has been well lived by me. The way to extinguishing has been well completed. I have seen with wisdom that existence is without any enjoyment. Therefore in my case, death is like a poison I have vomited.

711. The liberated one who doesn't have any attachment, who has crossed over saṁsāra, and who reached the far shore, delights in the end of life when the time of living has ended. He feels like one released from execution. (For Arahants, carrying on in saṁsāra is like awaiting execution.)

712. The one who attained liberation doesn't long for anything in the world. This is a natural law. He is like someone who jumped out of a burning house. He doesn't grieve at death.

713. Whatever conditioned thing there is in the world, whatever existence there is, all of that is out of control, non-self. So it has been said by the Great Seer, the Buddha.

714. Whoever understands this as it was taught by the Buddha doesn't take hold of any existence. For him, existence appears to be a blazing, heated iron ball.

715. I don't have the thought "I was in the past." Nor do I have the thought, "I shall be in the future." All conditioned things are changing. So, in this case why should I lament?

716. Dear leader of the thieves, clearly life means a formation of causes and effects that gives rise to suffering—dependant arising. Clearly, life means the continuity of conditioned things. There is no fear for one who sees this reality.

717. When by developed wisdom one sees this life, it appears to be like grass and a pile of wood to him. He doesn't gain anything to hold on to as "mine." For such a person, there is nothing to grieve thinking, "Oh, I am going to lose what is mine."

718. I have indeed become disenchanted with my body. I don't have anything to do with this existence. This body is nothing but fragile. I don't need another body again.

719. Now, if you have any use for this body, do whatever you want. (Kill me if you please.) As a result, I won't have any reason to hate or to love.

720. Hearing the strange words of the liberated monk, the thieves couldn't believe their eyes; they were shocked with hair standing on end. Right there, they threw their swords away and said to the liberated monk:

721. [Thieves:] Great sage, who is indeed your teacher? Whose teaching did you hear to live without sorrow like this? Whose path did you enter?

722. [Arahant Adhimutta:] My great teacher is someone who has realized everything that should be realized. He is someone who conquered the whole world. He is someone who has great compassion. He is someone who knows everything. That Blessed One is my teacher. My great teacher is the superb physician who heals the world with the medicine of Dhamma.

723. The Supreme Buddha taught me the unsurpassed Dhamma which leads to the destruction of all suffering. I entered that Dhamma path and obtained this sorrowless life.

724. Having heard the Dhamma of the Great Seer, those thieves threw away their swords and weapons. Some of the thieves stopped stealing completely and became virtuous. Some others became monks and illuminated the Buddha's community of disciples. (They became enlightened ones.)

725. Having become monks under the guidance of the Buddha, those wise monks developed enlightenment factors and spiritual powers. Meditating with joyful minds, they gained wisdom. Based on developed spiritual faculties, they went beyond cause and effect condition. They attained the Supreme bliss of Nibbāna.

These verses were said by Arahant Adhimutta.

The Verses of Arahant Pārāsariya

726. The monk Pārāsariya is a meditator. When he was seated alone, secluded, these thoughts came into his mind:

727. As a human, one should work for one's own benefit. He should act without harming others. What should be his duties? What should be his behaviour?

728. A human's sense bases can be used for his welfare or his harm. If he doesn't guard his senses, they will surely lead to harm. If he guards his senses, they will certainly lead to happiness.

729. Therefore, the one who acts for his own good and the one who doesn't harm others should protect his faculties well and handle them properly.

730. When his eyes chase after beautiful forms, if he does not understand the danger of that unrestraint, he won't be able to escape from suffering.

731. When his ears chase after beautiful sounds, if he does not understand the danger of that unrestraint, he won't be able to escape from suffering.

732. Not knowing about the removal of desire, if he smells things, being caught up with sweet fragrances, he won't be able to escape from suffering.

733. If he recollects flavours thinking this is bitter, this is sweet, and this is sour, his mind will be tied by craving for taste. He won't be able to understand the nature of this mind.

734. If he recollects tangibles thinking this is lovely and is pleasant to touch, his mind will become attached to it. As a result, when lust invades his mind, he will have to suffer with various pains.

735. When mind objects enter his mind, if he is unable to guard his mind from those objects, he will have to suffer because of all the five senses.

736. This body is like a beautiful and attractive painted pot made by a skillful artist, but it is filled with puss, blood and a lot of filth.

737. Life is like something bitter with sweet enjoyment, a painful thing which has a pleasant attachment. The one who doesn't understand this lives like one who licks a razor smeared with honey.

738. If a man is passionately attached to the form of a woman, the sound of a woman, the touch of a woman, and the scent of a woman, he will have to suffer with various pains.

739. These aspects of a woman flow into a man's thought like a rapid stream. But if he can stop that rapid stream, he is a great hero.

740. He is the one who achieves goodness, and lives by the Dhamma. He is a wise and skillful person. Even if he is a lay person, he will reach goodness righteously.

741. Even as a lay person, he doesn't engage in unbeneficial things. Understanding the things clearly that shouldn't be done, he acts wisely and diligently.

742. One should practice whatever is connected with goodness and whatever pleasure is produced by wholesome qualities. The combination of these truly is the supreme happiness.

743. Some people desire to take others' belongings by cheating them. Such people even having killed, beaten, and inflicted suffering on them try to forcefully grab their belongings.

744. The wise person knocks out desire for senses using those same senses. It is like a strong person who knocks out one peg with another peg.

745. Such a wise person develops the Five Spiritual Faculties: faith, effort, mindfulness, one-pointedness of mind and wisdom. With these five developed faculties, he strikes the five senses. Indeed he is a Brāhmin who is freed from suffering.

746. That noble person has achieved the true goal of life and has become established in the Dhamma. Having acted according to the words of the Supreme Buddha, he has realized everything. He has prospered in supreme happiness.

These verses were said by Arahant Pārāsariya.

The Verses of Arahant Telakāni

747. I was truly very energetic. For a long time I went about searching for the Dhamma. I inquired from many recluses and brāhmins. But I didn't get to hear a true Dhamma which calms the mind.

748. Who indeed crossed over the world? Who is the person who has attained Nibbāna? Whose Dhamma should I accept for realizing the truth of this life?

749. Those days, I was inwardly cunning. Like a fish that has swallowed bait, like the asura Vepacitta bound by the snare of God Sakka, I was bound by defilements.

750. Then I was removing those defilements but still I was unable to get rid of grief and lamentation. Who in this world could teach me a Dhamma giving realization to release me from these bonds?

751. Who is that recluse or brāhmin who could teach me a Dhamma that destroys defilements? From whom should I accept a Dhamma that washes away old age and death?

752. I led a life which was tied together with uncertainty and doubt, powered by arrogance, boiled by anger, stiffened by pride and sunken in desires.

753. There is a bow made of craving. There are about thirty arrows called views that came from that bow. See how they have penetrated to the depth of the heart!

754. There are these false theories which are used to win arguments. Since I clung to them and did not abandon them, I was destroyed by those very same wrong views. I trembled like a leaf shaken by the wind.

755. This life with its sense bases was completely entangled in the view of self. That is why I trembled so much.

756. I did not meet anyone who could cure me by removing the dart of defilements from me with a knife, or other cutting tools.

757. Without using a knife, and without injuring, who could remove these darts of defilements which have pierced my mind all over?

758. I had fallen into a great danger. Removing the poison of defilements with the Dhamma, if someone could give me his hand, truly he becomes the best for me.

759. I was drowned in a lake filled with deceit, conceit, arrogance and sleepiness. My body was permanently covered with the mud of defilement.

760. My life was filled with the thunder of conceit and clouds of fetters. I was carried here and there by the winds of wrong views and intentions of desires.

761. The stream of craving flows throughout all the sense bases. Craving is tangled in life like a vine wrapped around a tree. Who could block this stream of craving? Who could cut this creeper of craving?

762. Good man, make a dam to block the stream of craving. May you not fall into hell from this stream of mind-born defilements, like a tree falls from the rapid current.

763. Indeed I was very scared. I was seeking the way to go to the far shore from the near shore. Finally I met the great protection, the great teacher who has the weapons of wisdom, surrounded by Great Seers.

764. My great teacher held out a pure, beautiful staircase for me. It is made out of the hardwood called true Dhamma. Since I was carried away by the stream of defilements, my great teacher asked me to climb the staircase saying, "Cross over! Don't be afraid."

765-66. Then I climbed the Dhamma tower called mindfulness. Having climbed there, I wisely investigated the true nature of life. Whatever I previously delighted in, clinging to self centered view, all of that, I abandoned. I saw the way to get on the ship heading to Nibbāna. Having abandoned the view of self, I saw the supreme shore, Nibbāna.

767. The Supreme Buddha taught a supreme way that leads to the complete cessation of the darts of defilements produced by links of existences.

768. The Buddha is the greatest remover of the poison of defilements. For a long time there were those knots of defilements that surrounded the depth of my heart. My great teacher cast off all those knots for me.

These verses were said by Arahant Telakāni.

The Verses of Arahant Raṭṭhapāla

769. See the true nature of this body which is created by putting together tendons and bones, even though it seems to be like a beautiful painted puppet. Foolish people delight in and appreciate this body. This body is subject to diseases and doesn't have any permanent stability.

770. One should see the true nature of this body even though it is decorated with jewels and ornaments. This skeleton wrapped up in skin is made attractive by its clothes.

771. The feet are painted with colours and the mouth produces fragrances having chewed mint. These things are enough to trick a fool but do nothing for one who seeks Nibbāna.

772. The hair is braided stylishly, and the eyes are painted with makeup. These things are enough to trick a fool but do nothing for one who seeks Nibbāna.

773. This filthy body is kept as a nicely decorated pot. This is enough to trick a fool but does nothing for one who seeks Nibbāna.

774. The deer hunter set out the traps, but the deer did not get caught by the trap. While the deer trapper was lamenting, having eaten the bait, we left quickly.

775. The hunter's trap was smashed, but the deer didn't get caught. While the deer trapper was crying, having eaten the bait, we left quickly.

776. I have seen the wealthy people in this world. When they obtain wealth, they become deluded. They don't give it away to anybody. Having gathered wealth greedily, they desire more and more sensual pleasures.

777. A king who has conquered all the land on this shore and rules over the ocean-bound world is still unsatisfied. He hungers to rule over a country even beyond the ocean.

778. That king and many other people die with craving. They give up their life unsatisfied. There is no satisfaction in this world from sensual pleasures.

779. When someone dies their relatives, with messy hair, mourn over them. They say, "Oh, may our relative become immortal!" Then they carry the dead body out, wrap it in a cloth, place it on a pile of wood and burn it.

780. Leaving his entire wealth, wrapped in a single cloth and poked by spears, he burns. When he dies, neither his relatives nor his friends can protect him.

781. Heirs take his wealth. He went on his journey after death according to his actions but his wealth does not follow him, nor does his wife, children or country.

782. One does not obtain long life by wealth, nor does one escape from old age by riches. That is why wise sages say that this life is short, non-eternal and subject to change.

783. The rich and the poor both feel the contact of senses through objects. The wise and the fool both feel the contact of senses through objects. But the fool, due to his lack of wisdom, suffers by that contact and sleeps uncomfortably. The wise sage is not shaken by any contact.

784. Therefore it is very clear that wisdom is better than wealth. It is through this very wisdom one can end suffering. But the beings who have clung to this existence commit evil deeds due to their delusion.

785. After death they again fall into saṁsāra, suffering. They come again into a womb. Those who approve of others' misdeeds also fall into the same tragedy.

786. A thief who is caught suffers because of his own evil deed. In the same way, beings suffer in the next world because of their own evil deeds.

787. Dear king, it is true that these sensual pleasures are sweet, delightful and attractive. But they disturb the mind by their various forms. Having understood this danger of sensual pleasures, I became a monk.

788. Just as the fruits on a tree will fall, so everyone, young or old, will die. Dear king, having seen this suffering, I became a monk. Certainly this monk life is better.

789. I became a monk out of faith. I entered the path of the Buddha with confidence. My monk life is not without result. I eat my alms free from debt.

790. I understood sensual pleasures to be like a huge blazing fire. I understood all valuables such as gold and silver to be like weapons. I understood suffering from entry into the womb and the great fearfulness of hells.

791. I realized this danger. I was completely shocked. Previously, I was beaten by the arrows of defilements. But now, having eradicated all defilements, I have become an enlightened one.

792. The Great Teacher's instruction has been respectfully followed by me. The Buddha's path has been fully followed by me. I lowered the heavy load of defilements. I rooted out the fetter of existence.

793. I became a monk with the wish to achieve one goal. That, I have achieved. I have cut all fetters. I attained enlightenment.

These verses were said by Arahant Raṭṭhapāla.

The Verses of Arahant Māluṅkyaputta

794. When one sees a form with unestablished mindfulness, he recollects its pleasant signs. Then he experiences that form with an attached mind. His mind stays clinging to it.

795. Many feelings arise in him originating from that form. His mind is disturbed by desire and restlessness. For one who accumulates suffering in this way, Nibbāna is said to be far away.

796. When one hears a sound with unestablished mindfulness, he recollects its pleasant signs. Then he experiences that sound with an attached mind. His mind stays clinging to it.

797. Many feelings arise in him originating from that sound. His mind is disturbed by desire and restlessness. For one who accumulates suffering in this way, Nibbāna is said to be far away.

798. When one smells an odour with unestablished mindfulness, he recollects its pleasant signs. Then he experiences that odour with an attached mind. His mind stays clinging to it.

799. Many feelings arise in him originating from that odour. His mind is disturbed by desire and restlessness. For one who accumulates suffering in this way, Nibbāna is said to be far away.

800. When one tastes a flavour with unestablished mindfulness, he recollects its pleasant signs. Then he experiences that flavour with an attached mind. His mind clings to it.

801. Many feelings arise in him originating from that flavour. His mind is disturbed by desire and restlessness. For one who accumulates suffering in this way, Nibbāna is said to be far away.

802. When one feels a tangible with unestablished mindfulness, he recollects its pleasant signs. Then he experiences that tangible with an attached mind. His mind clings to it.

803. Many feelings arise in him originating from that tangible. His mind is disturbed by desire and restlessness. For one who accumulates suffering in this way, Nibbāna is said to be far away.

804. When one thinks a thought with unestablished mindfulness, he recollects its pleasant signs. Then he experiences that thought with an attached mind. His mind clings to it.

805. Many feelings arise in him originating from that thought. His mind is disturbed by desire and restlessness. For one who accumulates suffering in this way, Nibbāna is said to be far away.

806. When one sees a form with established mindfulness, he is not attached to that form. Then he experiences that form with a detached mind. His mind doesn't cling to it.

807. Through the way he sees that form and the way he associates with that feeling, defilements get destroyed. There is no accumulating. That is how he lives mindfully. For one who reduces suffering in this way, Nibbāna is said to be close by.

808. When one hears a sound with established mindfulness, he is not attached to that sound. Then he experiences that sound with a detached mind. His mind doesn't cling to it.

809. Through the way he hears that sound and the way he associates with that feeling, defilements get destroyed. There is no accumulating. That is how he lives mindfully. For one who reduces suffering in this way, Nibbāna is said to be close by.

810. When one smells an odour with established mindfulness, he is not attached to that odour. Then he experiences that odour with a detached mind. His mind doesn't cling to it.

811. Through the way he smells that odour and the way he associates with that feeling, defilements get destroyed. There is no

accumulating. That is how he lives mindfully. For one who reduces suffering, in this way Nibbāna is said to be close by.

812. When one tastes a flavour with established mindfulness, he is not attached to that flavour. Then he experiences that flavour with a detached mind. His mind doesn't cling to it.

813. Through the way he tastes that flavour and the way he associates with that feeling, defilements get destroyed. There is no accumulating. That is how he lives mindfully. For one who reduces suffering in this way, Nibbāna is said to be close by.

814. When one feels a tangible with established mindfulness, he is not attached to that tangible. Then he experiences that tangible with a detached mind. His mind doesn't cling to it.

815. Through the way he feels that tangible and the way he associates with that feeling, defilements get destroyed. There is no accumulating. That is how he lives mindfully. For one who reduces suffering in this way, Nibbāna is said to be close by.

816. When one thinks a thought with established mindfulness, he is not attached to that thought. Then he experiences that thought with a detached mind. His mind doesn't cling to it.

817. Through the way he thinks a thought and the way he associates with that feeling, defilements get destroyed. There is no accumulating. That is how he lives mindfully. For one who reduces suffering in this way, Nibbāna is said to be close by.

These verses were said by Arahant Māluṅkyaputta.

The Verses of Arahant Sela

818. [Brāhmin Sela:] Blessed One, with great energy, you have a perfect body. It is shining. You had a blessed birth, you are beautiful to look at, you have a golden body and you have pure white teeth.

819. A person who was born with great fortune, on his body there are great marks. I can see that all of those great marks are present on your body.

820. Your eyes are very beautiful, your face is very pleasant, and your well-built, straight body is like that of a Brahma. When you are in the midst of the community of monks, you shine like the sun.

821. Meritorious recluse, with this gold skin of yours you are very beautiful. When you have such supreme beauty, what is the use of this monkhood?

822. You are fit to be a powerful king in the land of India, a wheel turning monarch conquering the whole earth.

823. Then very powerful kings will attend on you. Rule the world oh Gotama, as the king of kings and as the lord of humans.

824. [The Blessed One:] Indeed dear Sela, I am a king. I am the Supreme Dhamma King. The Dhamma Wheel that I turn cannot be turned back by anyone in the world.

825. [Brāhmin Sela:] Meritorious Gotama, do you claim to be the incomparable Dhamma King, the Supremely Enlightened One? You say, "I turn the Dhamma wheel."

826. So then who is the Lord's general? Who is that disciple, the successor to the Teacher, who can turn the Dhamma Wheel exactly like you do?

827. [The Blessed One:] Dear Sela, following the example of the Tathāgatha, Sāriputta keeps the unsurpassed Dhamma wheel rolling that has been set rolling by me.

828. I realized everything that should be realized. I developed everything that should be developed. I eliminated everything that should be eliminated. Therefore, dear Brāhmin, I am the Buddha.

829. Dear Brāhmin, dispel your doubt in me. Have faith in me. It is extremely rare to obtain again and again the sight of a supremely enlightened Buddha.

830. I am the Supreme Buddha. It is truly difficult to often have the appearance of such a rare being in the world. Dear Brāhmin, I am an unsurpassed Dhamma surgeon.

831. I have attained the most supreme state. I am unbeatable. I defeated the army of Māra. Having overcome all enemy powers, I live happily seeing no fear from any direction.

832. [Brāhmin Sela:] Dear pupils, listen to these beautiful words of the Great Sage, the one with the eyes of Dhamma. He is a superb surgeon who removes the darts of defilements from the hearts of living beings. He's a great hero. He is like a lion king roaring in the forest.

833. He has become the most supreme. He's unbeatable. He has won the battle against the army of Māra. Having seen such a great teacher, who wouldn't have faith except those born with little merit?

834. I will become a monk in the presence of the Supreme Buddha, the one with excellent wisdom. If you would also like to become monks with me, do so. If you don't want to, then go back.

835. [Pupils:] Dear teacher, if the path of the fully enlightened Buddha is that pleasing to you, we would also like to be pleased by this. We would like to become monks in the presence of the Supreme Buddha, the one with excellent wisdom.

836. [Brāhmin Sela:] Blessed One, here there are three hundred brāhmins. Worshiping you, they all ask for the holy life from you. We would all like to practice the holy life in the Blessed One's presence.

837. [The Blessed One:] Dear Sela, I have proclaimed the holy life very well. This Dhamma is to be understood in this very life. This

Dhamma can be understood anytime. If you practice diligently as I teach, your monk life won't be in vain.

838. [Arahant Sela:] Sage with eyes of Dhamma, Supreme Buddha, this is the eighth day since we went for refuge to the Triple Gem. Blessed One, in seven days we all have been tamed by your excellent instruction.

839. Indeed, you are the Supreme Buddha. You are the excellent teacher. You are the Great Sage who overcame Māra. Cutting off all defilements, you crossed over samsāra and now you have also helped us to cross over.

840. You have crossed over all defilements. You have destroyed the taints. You have eliminated all fears. You have eradicated clinging. Truly, you are like a brave lion.

841. These three hundred monks are worshiping you with joined palms. Great hero, please stretch out your feet. Let these noble beings pay homage to the Supreme Teacher's sacred feet!

These verses were said by Arahant Sela.

The Verses of Arahant Bhaddiya

842. I used to ride on an elephant's back. I used to wear very soft clothes. I used to eat delicious white rice and meat curry.

843. But now I am very fortunate. Today, I lead the life of a recluse energetically delighted with my alms round. Bhaddiya, son of Kāligodha, meditates without clinging.

844. He is satisfied with the life of wearing rag robes and is delighted with his alms round. Bhaddiya, son of Kāligodha, meditates without clinging.

845. He is satisfied with the life of begging for food and is delighted with his alms round. Bhaddiya, son of Kāligodha, meditates without clinging.

846. He is satisfied with the life of wearing the triple robe and is delighted with his alms round. Bhaddiya, son of Kāligodha, meditates without clinging.

847. He is satisfied with the life of going on the begging round to every house without exception and is delighted with his alms round. Bhaddiya, son of Kāligodha, meditates without clinging.

848. He is satisfied with the life of eating only one meal a day and is delighted with his alms round. Bhaddiya, son of Kāligodha, meditates without clinging.

849. He is satisfied with the life of eating only from the alms bowl and is delighted with his alms round. Bhaddiya, son of Kāligodha, meditates without clinging.

850. He is satisfied with the life of never accepting anything more after he accepted food to his bowl and is delighted with his alms round. Bhaddiya, son of Kāligodha, meditates without clinging.

851. He is satisfied with the life of living in the forest and is delighted with his alms round. Bhaddiya, son of Kāligodha, meditates without clinging.

852. He is satisfied with the life of living at the foot of a tree and is delighted with his alms round. Bhaddiya, son of Kāligodha, meditates without clinging.

853. He is satisfied with the life of living in the open air and is delighted with his alms round. Bhaddiya, son of Kāligodha, meditates without clinging.

854. He is satisfied with the life of living in a cemetery and is delighted with his alms round. Bhaddiya, son of Kāligodha, meditates without clinging.

855. He is satisfied with the life of using any seat that is there for him and is delighted with his alms round. Bhaddiya, son of Kāligodha, meditates without clinging.

856. He is satisfied with the life of meditating in the night without sleeping and is delighted with his alms round. Bhaddiya, son of Kāligodha, meditates without clinging.

857. He is satisfied with the life of few wishes and is delighted with his alms round. Bhaddiya, son of Kāligodha, meditates without clinging.

858. He is satisfied with the life of being contented with whatever is available and is delighted with his alms round. Bhaddiya, son of Kāligodha, meditates without clinging.

859. He is satisfied with the life of living in seclusion and is delighted with his alms round. Bhaddiya, son of Kāligodha, meditates without clinging.

860. He is satisfied with the life of not being attached to anything and is delighted with his alms round. Bhaddiya, son of Kāligodha, meditates without clinging.

861. He is satisfied with the life of continuing his effort and is delighted with his alms round. Bhaddiya, son of Kāligodha, meditates without clinging.

862. Previously, I used a beautifully fashioned, valuable golden bowl. I gave it up. I replaced it with a clay bowl. This is my second crowning.

863. Previously, I lived in the top floor of a palace. There was a tall wall circling my city. There was an army with swords in their hands to guard me. But still, I lived full of fear.

864. Today, this Bhaddiya lives without any fear or agitation. Bhaddiya, son of Kāligodha, having gone into the forest, meditates.

865. He became an enlightened one standing firm in great virtue, developing mindfulness, wisdom and gradually destroying all fetters.

These verses were said by Arahant Bhaddiya.

The Verses of Arahant Aṅgulimāla

866. [Aṅgulimāla:] Hey recluse, while you are walking you tell me you have stopped. But now when I have stopped, you say I have not stopped. I ask you now recluse, what is the meaning of this? How is it that you have stopped and I have not?

867. [Buddha:] Aṅgulimāla, this is how I have stopped. I have stopped harming beings forever. I abstain from violence towards living beings. But this is how you have not stopped. You have no sympathy towards beings. Therefore I have stopped and you have not.

868. [Aṅgulimāla:] Oh, you are truly a sacred recluse, a Great Seer. Out of compassion for me, you have come to this great forest. Having heard your stanza teaching me the Dhamma, I am changed. Indeed I will abandon my evil ways forever.

869. Saying so, the robber threw his sword and other weapons off the mountain. He knelt down at the Blessed One's sacred feet and worshiped him. On that very spot, he pleaded to the Supreme Buddha to become a monk.

870. The Buddha is the most compassionate seer. He shows the way to Nibbāna to the whole world along with its gods. The Buddha addressed Aṅgulimāla saying, "Come, monk." That was Aṅgulimāla's ordination.

871. The one who is negligent in practicing the Dhamma before but afterwards practices the Dhamma diligently, he illuminates this world like the moon freed from the clouds.

872. If someone closes off his evil actions by the power of wholesome deeds, he illuminates this world like the moon freed from the clouds.

873. Even though a monk is very young, if he practises virtue, concentration and wisdom, he illuminates this world like the moon freed from the clouds.

874. May even my enemies hear this Dhamma. Let even my enemies follow the Buddha's path. Let even my enemies associate with noble people who promote this excellent Dhamma.

875. May even my enemies hear that excellent Dhamma of those noble ones who praise patience and kindness! Let them follow that excellent Dhamma!

876. May those enemies of mine not harm me or anyone else! Now Aṅgulimāla has attained the highest peace. He protects both frightened beings and fearless enlightened ones.

877. Canal makers guide the water in whatever direction they need. Arrow makers straighten out arrows. Carpenters straighten out the timber as they wish. In the same way, wise people tame their lives.

878. Some people tame other beings with sticks, hooks or whips, but without sticks or weapons I was tamed by the great Buddha who has an unshaken mind.

879. Previously "Harmless" was my name even though at that time I was harming others. But now I am truly harmless since I don't harm anyone at all.

880. Formerly, I was the famous serial killer, wearer of the finger garland, Aṅgulimāla. While I was being swept along in the great flood of saṁsāra, I got to go for refuge to the Buddha.

881. Formerly I was famous, known as the bloody handed Aṅgulimāla. But see the benefit of my going to refuge to the Supreme Triple Gem! I cut off all links of existence at their roots.

882. I did many evil deeds leading to rebirth in hell. But I experience their results only in this life. So I eat my alms free from debt.

883. Foolish people waste their whole lives doing useless things. They forget the Dhamma practice. But wise people guard the diligent Dhamma practice like someone protecting a great treasure.

884. Don't be negligent to practice the Dhamma. Don't seek delight in sensual pleasures. The one who meditates with diligence reaches the Supreme bliss.

885. How good it is that I entered the Buddha's path! It is not something unbeneficial. What I'm saying is nothing but the truth. Through the well analysed Dhamma, I attained the very best, Nibbāna.

886. How beneficial it is that I entered the Buddha's path! It is not something unbeneficial. What I'm saying is nothing but the truth. I have attained the Triple Knowledge. The Buddha's path has been fully followed by me.

887. Formerly, either in the forest, at the foot of a tree or in the mountain caves—everywhere—I lived with an agitated mind.

888. But now I sleep happily. I stand happily. I live my life happily. I jumped out from Māra's snare. Ah! How much compassion my great teacher gave me!

889. Formerly, I was born into a high-born brāhmin family, pure on both mother's and father's side. But now I am the son of the King of the Dhamma, the unique teacher, the Supreme Buddha.

890. Now I don't have any craving nor do I have any clinging. I am restrained with guarded senses. I eliminated the root of suffering. Destroying all taints, I became an enlightened one.

891. The Buddha's instruction has been respectfully followed by me. The Buddha's path has been fully followed by me. I lowered the heavy load of defilements. I rooted out the fetters of existence.

These verses were said by Arahant Aṅgulimāla.

The Verses of Arahant Anuruddha

892. If he left his mother, father, sisters and brothers, relatives and the five cords of sensual pleasures, he should meditate like this Anuruddha does.

893. Formerly, I was surrounded by songs and dance. I woke from sleep to the sound of music. I was trapped in Māra's snare of sensual pleasures, but I didn't gain any purity from that.

894. Giving up these sensual pleasures, delighting in the Buddha's path and crossing over all the floods of defilements, one should meditate like this Anuruddha does.

895. Forms, sounds, smells, tastes, and touches are attractive. Removing desire for them, one should meditate like this Anuruddha does.

896. After returning from alms round, the sage lives alone. He doesn't have the companion called "craving." Freed from taints, Anuruddha is searching for a thrown away rag.

897. He has clear mindfulness. Taintless sage, Anuruddha found a thrown away rag. He washed it well and dyed it. He wore that as a robe.

898. Having many desires, without being content with what is available, and mingling with the crowd, if one lives with a conceited mind, all of these behaviours generate evil defilements in him.

899–900. But establishing clear mindfulness, desiring little, being contented with what is available, if one lives energetically, with a still mind, all of these behaviours become aids to enlightenment. The Great Seer, the Buddha, spoke about that person as a taintless one.

901. The unsurpassed teacher in the world knew my thoughts and, by his psychic powers, creating a mind made body, approached me.

902. My great teacher beautifully explained more about the things I was thinking. The Supreme Buddha, delighting in Nibbāna, taught me about Nibbāna.

903. Having learned the Buddha's Dhamma, I delighted in his path. I achieved the Triple Knowledge. The Buddha's path has been fully followed by me.

904. It has been fifty-five years since I started meditating without sleep. It has been twenty-five years since sleepiness was abandoned completely.

905. The Buddha had an unshaken mind and was established in Nibbāna. The Blessed One's breathing in and breathing out halted. The Great Sage with eyes of Dhamma who was freed from craving, aiming at serene Nibbāna, attained final extinguishing at passing away.

906. The Blessed One had an unstirred mind and endured all feelings with that mind. His mind was released from craving. That liberated mind was extinguished like a lamp.

907. Now what remains here is only the five faculties of the Great sage's final body. Once a supremely enlightened Buddha has attained final extinguishing, nothing will remain.

908. Hey, net of craving! I too now don't have any living, even in a heaven. Journeying on from rebirth to rebirth has completely ended. There is no more rebirth.

909. He can know in an instant about thousands of worlds along with the Brahma World. He has psychic powers and the knowledge of seeing the death and rebirth of beings. Devas also visit this monk at the proper time.

910. In a former life, he was very poor. His job was carrying leftover food. His name was Annabhāra. He suffered a lot. At that time, there was a private Buddha named Upariṭṭha who was well known. He made an offering to that Buddha.

911. In this life, I was born in the Sākya clan. Everybody knew me as Anuruddha. I was surrounded by music and dance. I woke up from my sleep listening to music.

912. One day I saw the fully enlightened teacher, the Supreme Buddha who was without fear from any direction. My heart was pleased with him. Then I abandoned my home life and became a monk.

913. I achieved the knowledge to see my former lives in saṁsāra. I have been born hundreds of times in the Tāvatiṁsa Heaven.

914. Seven times I have become a universal wheel turning king and have ruled this whole earth bounded by the ocean. I have ruled the world as the great king of the Indian subcontinent righteously without stick or sword.

915. Having passed from the human world, I was reborn in heaven seven times. Having passed from heaven, I was reborn in the human world seven times. Even as a God, I had the knowledge of past lives.

916. The fourth Jhāna is very peaceful. The mind gets very unified and tranquil there very well. Using this, I purified my divine eye.

917. Using the fourth Jhāna, I also understood the death and rebirth of beings according to their kamma.

918. The Buddha's instruction has been respectfully followed by me. The Buddha's path has been fully followed by me. I lowered the heavy load of defilements. I rooted out the fetters of existence.

919. I live in the village of Beluva in the Vajji country. My life is just about to end. Under the shade of these bamboo trees, with a taintless mind, I will attain final extinguishing at passing away.

These verses were said by Arahant Anuruddha.

The Verses of Arahant Pārāsariya

920. Flowers have blossomed throughout the forest where there was a monk with a still mind. While he was meditating in seclusion, this thought came to him:

921. The behaviour of the monks at present is different from when the protector of the world, the best of men, the Buddha, was alive.

922. Those days monks used robes as a protection from the wind, as a covering for their private parts, and to be content with whatever was available.

923. In the past, no matter what kind of food they were given, whether it was delicious or bad, little or much, monks were not greedy and did not cling to it, they ate alms just to stay alive.

924. In the past, when they were sick, rather than searching for medicine they worked hard for the abandonment of taints.

925. In forests, at the foot of trees, near waterfalls, and in caves, devoting themselves to seclusion, in the past, monks lived making seclusion their aim.

926. Those monks were obedient. They were easy to support. They were gentle. They had unstubborn minds. They weren't involved in disputes. Their words were not scattered. They lived very meaningful lives thinking about their goal.

927. Therefore, their stride, eating, and association were pleasing. Their postures were smooth, like a stream of oil.

928. Those noble disciples practiced Jhānas, eradicated all taints and were very compassionate. Now those enlightened ones have attained final extinguishing at passing away. Now there are few such noble monks.

929. If the development of wholesome qualities and path for gaining wisdom are abandoned, this perfect path of the Buddha will disappear from the world.

930. At a time when evil things and defilements have taken over, even if one practices a secluded life, one will gain only a learning of the Dhamma.

931. Those increasing defilements will eat up all humans. As a result, nothing else will happen but those defilements will sport with people. It is something like a group of crazy people who live with demons.

932. Defilements will overcome those people. Then they will run here and there searching for objects of sensual pleasures. It will seem like a squad of soldiers who just received commands.

933. Then, true Dhamma will be abandoned. They will start quarreling with each other. They will follow after wrong views thinking that they are important.

934. Even though they become monks having given up wealth, wives and sons, they will do things that shouldn't be done even just for the sake of food.

935. Then, they will eat food until they are overfull and sleep lying on their backs. After they have woken up, they will waste their time by talking about gossip that was condemned by the great teacher.

936. Their minds won't be internally calm. They will eagerly learn unnecessary things. The Supreme Dhamma leading to the development of monkhood will be abandoned.

937. They will delight in getting things from people. So with the intention of getting more things in return, they will give lay people clay, oil, powder, water, seats and food.

938. They will also give tooth cleaners, fruits, flowers, deserts, mangos and myrobalans. Eventually, they will even give food that they get on alms round.

939. After that, those monks will start giving medicine to people like doctors. They will spend life like ordinary lay people. They

will decorate their bodies like prostitutes. They will collect luxurious items like a king.

940. They will cheat others by telling lies. Living a cunning life, they will use other people's things unrighteously.

941. They will promote unallowable things as allowable. Aiming at luxurious lives, they will cheat people and get things for their own benefit.

942. They will receive special treatment from lay people, not righteously, but pretending that it is a meritorious project. They will teach the Dhamma to others not to explain the meaning but to gain things in return.

943. In reality, they don't belong to the Noble Sanga but they will quarrel to get things that are offered to the real Noble Sangha. They indeed live on others' gains. They are not ashamed of their wrong living. They are shameless.

944. Not following the true monkhood, some fake monks will shave their heads well and wear double robes. Being intoxicated by gains and special care, they will desire to get respect from others.

945. As a result, the Dhamma path will crumble. Noble disciples who achieved Jhānas and Dhamma realization won't be found anymore. Achieving and protecting noble qualities such as Jhānas and higher knowledges is not easy.

946. One should walk very carefully on thorny ground. In the same way, a sage should go in a village establishing strong mindfulness.

947. Therefore, one should remember the lives of the enlightened ones who lived in the past. One should recollect how they lived. At least in the final stage of one's life, if one follows the Noble Path, he can attain Nibbāna.

948. After speaking these verses, that liberated monk, who eradicated rebirth—the true Seer, the true Brāhmin who developed spiritual faculties—attained final extinguishing at passing away in the Sāla forest.

These verses were said by Arahant Pārāsariya.

Section of Thirty Verses

The Verses of Arahant Phussa

949. There was an ascetic called Paṇḍaragotta. He saw many monks who were pleasing to see. Their senses were very calm. They had developed minds. The Ascetic Paṇḍaragotta asked the Arahant Phussa about them.

950. [Paṇḍaragotta:] Please answer my question. What are the desires going to be for the monks in the future? What would be their goal? What would be their attitude?

951. [Phussa Bhante:] Ascetic Paṇḍara, then listen to me. I will tell you what is going to happen in the future. Memorize it well.

952. In the future, the monks will often get angry and will be full of hatred. They will take revenge and destroy others' good qualities. Swollen with conceit, they will boast about qualities that are not present in themselves. They will envy others and argue with them.

953. With a conceited mind, they will mistakenly think that they know the deep Dhamma. They will just brag. But in reality they have no idea about the Dhamma. They are fickle. They won't have any respect towards the Supreme Dhamma nor will they have any respect towards each other.

954. Like this, many dangers will appear in the future world. These people will defile the well taught Supreme Dhamma with various wrong views.

955. In the future these monks will be powerful. They will be the leaders of the community of monks. But they will be devoid of virtuous qualities. They will be incompetent in the Dhamma. The

truth is that they won't know the teaching of the Buddha but will only just talk.

956. In the community of the monks there will be monks with good qualities who have a good understanding of the Dhamma and who fear to do wrong. But those virtuous monks will not stand out and will be powerless.

957. What will those evil monks devoid of wisdom do? They will accept silver and gold, fields, properties, goats and sheep, and male and female servants.

958. They won't have any wisdom, virtue or stillness of mind. Being conceited they will just boast. They will wander about like animals looking for quarrels to pick.

959. Wearing blue robes, monks in the future will lead conceited, deceitful, and stubborn lives. Living playfully, they will pretend to be noble ones.

960. In the future monks will wear white robes too. They will slick their hair back with oil. They will travel on roads, eyes painted with makeup.

961. They will desire the white robe and will dislike the dyed robes known as the Banner of the enlightened ones, the robes that were worn and praised by liberated ones.

962. They will be desirers of gain. They will be lazy and devoid of energy. They will give up living in faraway forests and meditating in secluded places. Instead they will stay close to villages.

963. They will live by wrong livelihood. Without training their students for a restrained life, while obtaining gains, they will train their pupils for a lifestyle dedicated to gaining things.

964. Those monks who won't obtain gains, honor, fame and praise will be forgotten without having any recognition. Even though there will be some virtuous and wise monks, without having any gains, no one will associate with them.

965. The Noble monk's banner is the robe which is dyed by the stain of the bark of the black banyan tree. But future monks will despise that robe and wear white clothes, the symbol of other religious people.

966. Once they have no reverence for the dyed robe, they will also give up the reflection on using the robe.

967. Having got hit with a poisoned spear, even though that elephant king Chaddanta was feeling terrible, unbearable pain, he respected this sacred dyed robe.

968. That day the elephant king Chaddanta, seeing the dyed robe, the banner of liberated ones, immediately said these meaningful verses:

969. Even though a person who hasn't eradicated defilements and is devoid of sense restraint and truth wears a dyed robe, surely he doesn't deserve that robe.

970. If a monk who has eradicated defilements, is virtuous, still minded, with self-restraint and truth, and wears a dyed robe, indeed he is the one who deserves this robe.

971. Devoid of virtue, foolish, acting impulsively, with a confused mind, and without wholesome qualities, such a person does not deserve this dyed robe.

972. But the one who is virtuous, desireless, still minded and with pure intentions deserves this dyed robe.

973. If one is stubborn, swollen with conceit, devoid of any knowledge and virtue, he truly deserves white clothes. What good will the dyed robe do for him?

974. In the future both monks and nuns will live with corrupt and disrespectful minds. They will insult even the enlightened ones whose minds are unshaken and full of loving kindness.

975. Even though virtuous monks will try to train those foolish people who are devoid of virtue and wisdom, unrestrained, and who act emotionally, they will still be ignored.

976. That is how they will live, without respecting each other or their teachers, as a disobedient horse to its rider.

977. When the period of disciplined monks and nuns comes to an end, these behaviours will appear in the future.

978. Before this very fearful future comes, be obedient to the Dhamma and have soft and unconceited hearts. Live respecting others!

979. Develop a mind of loving kindness and live a compassionate life. Restrained with virtue, putting forth energy, and giving top priority to the Dhamma practice, live with strong effort!

980. Negligence in regard to the Dhamma should be seen as a fearful thing. Diligence in the practice should be seen as a safe land. Develop the Noble Eightfold Path wishing to attain the deathless Nibbāna!

These verses were said by Arahant Phussa.

The Verses of Arahant Sāriputta

981. If a monk is virtuous, is full of mindfulness, meditates with restrained thoughts, practices the Dhamma diligently, delights in meditation, is still internally, and is content living in seclusion, he is truly called a monk.

982. Whether the food he eats is moist or dry, he doesn't overeat. He keeps some empty space in his stomach. A monk should eat mindfully knowing the limit. That is how a monk should live.

983. Without eating the last four or five mouthfuls, he should fill his stomach with water. This leads to the comfort of a monk who is diligent in reaching Nibbāna.

984. He should wear an allowable robe just to cover the private parts of his body. This leads to the comfort of a monk who is diligent in reaching Nibbāna.

985. As he sits for meditation, as long as his knees don't get wet from the rain, such a hut will do for a monk. This leads to the comfort of a monk who is diligent in reaching Nibbāna.

986. If one sees happy feelings as pain, painful feelings as a dart, and is not deluded by neutral feelings, then how could he be attached to this world?

987. There are people with evil desires, who are lazy, who lack Dhamma knowledge, and who are disrespectful. May I never have anything to do with such people. What good will come to this world by associating with them?

988. If one knows the supreme Dhamma well and is wise and virtuous, has a perfectly still mind, and is devoted to internal serenity—may that noble one stand right on my head.

989. The one who is sunk in and delights in sensual thoughts, angry thoughts, and thoughts of harming: he lives like a wild animal. That person misses the supreme Nibbāna, the end of suffering in saṁsāra.

990. But if one abandons those wrong thoughts without getting caught in wandering thoughts and delights in serene and insight meditation, he will attain the supreme Nibbāna, the end of suffering in saṁsāra.

991. Whether in a village or forest, on low ground or high ground, wherever the enlightened ones live, that land is indeed very delightful.

992. The seekers of sensual pleasures don't delight in forests. But the lust free sages who don't seek after sensual pleasures delight in the forests. They are truly excited about those forests.

993. One who notices your faults and corrects you is like someone who reveals a treasure. You should associate with such wise noble ones. Association with such wise noble ones always leads to good and never to bad.

994. He should advise, he should instruct, and he should restrain you from unwholesomeness. Such a person is dear to superior people, but not liked by evil people.

995. That day the Blessed Buddha, the one with eyes of Dhamma, was teaching the Dhamma to another person. While the Dhamma was being taught, being desirous towards realising the meaning, I was listening to it mindfully, paying full attention. My listening wasn't in vain. My mind was liberated from all taints and attained enlightenment.

996. I was not searching for the knowledge required to find my past lives, nor was I searching for the knowledge to obtain the divine eye, nor for the knowledge to read others' minds, nor for the knowledge to obtain psychic powers, nor for the knowledge of passing away and rebirth of beings, nor for the knowledge to obtain the divine ear.

997. With a shaven head, wearing the double robe, and sitting at the foot of a tree, he, liberated Upatissa, who became the foremost in wisdom, meditates.

998. The disciple of the fully enlightened Buddha has attained the Jhāna, devoid of applied thoughts, which is called noble silence.

999. A monk who abandoned delusion is unshaken, just like a firm, rocky mountain.

1000. To a person who is without defilements and always seeking purity, a hair's tip amount of evil seems as if it is the size of a cloud.

1001. I don't desire death, nor do I desire life, with clear mindfulness and awareness I will discard this body.

1002. I don't desire death nor do I desire life. Like a person who is waiting for his monthly salary, I am awaiting my time to attain final extinguishing at passing away.

1003. Either afterwards or before, on both sides there is death, not non-death. Therefore, follow only the Noble Eightfold Path. Do not perish! May this rare opportunity not pass you by.

1004. As a city is well guarded inside and out, so you should guard your life through the Dhamma. May this rare opportunity not pass you by. Many who missed this rare opportunity suffer, falling into hell.

1005. Be calm, abstain from evil, speak only with wise consideration, don't be conceited, and shakes off all evil things as the wind shakes a leaf off a tree.

1006. The monk who is calm abstains from evil, speaks only with wise consideration, and is not conceited, shakes off all evil things as the wind shakes a leaf off a tree.

1007. The monk who is ever calm, undisturbed by defilements, settled in mind, unstirred, full of good qualities and is wise can put an end to all suffering.

1008. One shouldn't have trust in some lay people and some monks as well because sometimes they are good but other times they become bad, and sometimes they are bad but other times they become good.

1009. Desire for sensual pleasures, anger, sloth and torpor, restlessness and remorse and doubt—these things defile the mind of a monk.

1010–11. But if a monk practices the Dhamma diligently and his one-pointedness of mind is not disturbed by either praise or blame, he practices Jhānas all the time, investigates even very subtle views with insight and delights in eradicating clinging; he is the one who can be called a superior person.

1012. Even the great ocean, the great earth, Mount Mahā Meru, and the great wind cannot be compared to the supreme liberation taught by the Great Teacher, the Buddha.

1013. With great wisdom, with a still mind, keeping the Buddha's Dhamma wheel rolling exactly how it was rolled by the Buddha, Sāriputta Bhante is like the great earth, water, and fire. He is not attached nor opposed to any object.

1014. Having attained the perfection of wisdom, having great wisdom, and having great mindfulness, that monk always lives quenched. Even though that monk is truly intelligent, he always lives as though he is unintelligent.

1015. The Buddha's instruction has been respectfully followed by me. The Buddha's path has been fully followed by me. I lowered the heavy load of defilements. I rooted out the fetters of existence.

1016. Follow the Noble Eightfold Path diligently. This is all I have to tell you. I was liberated from all existences. Now I am about to attain final extinguishing at passing away.

These verses were said by Arahant Sāriputta.

The Verses of Arahant Ānanda

1017. Some people have evil lives, breaking friendships using divisive speech, hating and envying others. A wise person doesn't like to make such people his friends. Association with evil people is also evil.

1018. There are people with faith in the Buddha, virtuous, wise, and well versed in the Dhamma. A wise person likes to make such people his friends. Associating with such superior people is indeed fortunate.

1019. See the true nature of this body which is created by putting together tendons and bones. Foolish people delight in and appreciate this body. This body is subject to diseases and doesn't have a permanent stability.

1020. Still, one should see the true nature of this body even though it is decorated with jewels and ornaments. This skeleton wrapped up in skin is made attractive by its clothes.

1021. The feet are painted with colours and the mouth produces fragrances having chewed mint. These things are enough to trick a fool but do nothing for one who seeks Nibbāna.

1022. The hair is braided stylishly, and the eyes are painted with makeup. These things are enough to trick a fool but do nothing for one who seeks Nibbāna.

1023. This filthy body is kept as a nicely decorated pot. This is enough to trick a fool but does nothing for one who seeks Nibbāna.

1024. The deer hunter set out the traps, but the deer did not get caught. While the deer trapper was crying, having eaten the bait, we left quickly.

1025. The hunter's trap was smashed. The deer didn't get caught. While the deer trapper was crying, having eaten the bait, we left quickly.

1026. Coming from the Gotama clan, with vast learning, this monk is a brilliant speaker of the Dhamma. He is the chief attendant of the Buddha. Having let down the burden of defilements, and having detached from all suffering, he lies down to sleep.

1027. That monk is free from taints, detached from all defilements and has overcome all ties, and he is indeed well quenched. Having crossed over the cycle of birth and death, he now bears his final body.

1028. In his heart he holds the teachings of the Buddha, the kinsman of the sun. This monk, Ānanda, from the clan of Gotama, is standing on the path leading to Nibbāna.

1029. I received eighty-two thousand Dhammas from the Buddha, and two thousand from the liberated monks. All together I memorized eighty-four thousand Dhammas.

1030. The person who is devoid of Dhamma knowledge grows like an ox. Only his flesh increases, not his wisdom.

1031. But on the other hand, if the person of great Dhamma knowledge tries to despise the one devoid of Dhamma knowledge using his own knowledge, it would seem to me as if a blind person were holding up a lamp.

1032. One should associate with a person of great Dhamma knowledge. Then one should not lose what one has heard already. That becomes a basis for this holy life. Therefore one should be an expert in the Dhamma.

1033. The one who knows to match the beginning and end of Dhamma phrases, understands its meaning well, and is skilled in analysing the meaning takes this Dhamma in the proper way. He also investigates the meaning with insight.

1034. When the Dhamma is applied to one's life, the desire for practicing the Dhamma arises. Then one practices Dhamma with full effort. He exerts himself in meditation and achieves perfect stillness of mind.

1035. The wise disciple who has a great knowledge of Dhamma and is an expert in the Dhamma always desires to obtain more Dhamma knowledge. One should associate with such disciples of the Buddha.

1036. That monk has great Dhamma knowledge, is an expert in the Dhamma, and is the guardian of the Great Seer's treasury. He is worthy of honour. He is like an eye for the whole world.

1037. The monk who lives in the Dhamma, delights in the Dhamma, recollects the Dhamma, and ponders the Dhamma does not fall away from the Dhamma.

1038. The person who cares about bodily happiness too much and is greedy for the body declines from the Dhamma when his body declines. If one desires the comfort of the body, how could he gain the comfort of the recluse's life?

1039. My noble friend is Sāriputta Bhante. When I heard that Sāriputta Bhante attained final extinguishing at passing away, I became disoriented. The Dhamma was not clear to me. I felt like the whole world sank in darkness.

1040. After my noble friends and my Great Teacher attained final extinguishing at their passing away, I no longer have any better friends than mindfulness of the body.

1041. Those old friends have passed away. I don't get along with the new friends. Therefore, I meditate all alone, like a bird gone to its nest to get away from the rain.

1042. Many people from various provinces are waiting to see me. Do not stop them from coming to me. May everyone who likes to listen to the Dhamma see me. Now is the time for that.

1043. Many people from various provinces came to see the Buddha. The Great Teacher allowed them to come to him. The one with eyes of Dhamma, the Buddha, did not stop them.

1044. For twenty-five years I lived as a trainee in this Dhamma. But still, even a thought of sensual pleasures didn't arise in me at all during that period. See the excellence of this Supreme Dhamma!

1045. For twenty-five years, I lived as a trainee in this Dhamma. But still, even a thought of anger didn't arise in me at all during that period. See the excellence of this Supreme Dhamma!

1046. For twenty-five years I served the Blessed One with bodily actions of loving kindness. I was always around him, just as his own shadow never left him.

1047. For twenty-five years I served the Blessed One with words of loving kindness. I was always around him, just as his own shadow never left him.

1048. For twenty-five years I served the Blessed One with thoughts of loving kindness. I was always around him, just as his own shadow never left him.

1049. While the Buddha was pacing up and down, I also paced up and down behind my Great Teacher. While the Buddha was preaching the Dhamma, knowledge arose in me.

1050. Still I am a trainee in this path. I still haven't attained enlightenment. I still have more tasks to complete. But my Great Teacher, who was very sympathetic to me, is about to attain final extinguishing at his passing away.

1051. When the Supreme Buddha, who possessed all excellent qualities, attained final extinguishing at passing away, the whole world, with hair standing on end was shaken with terror.

1052. Venerable Ānanda was the guardian of the Great Seer, the Buddha's treasury of Dhamma. He had a wide knowledge of Dhamma, like an eye for the whole world. He too attained final extinguishing at passing away.

1053. The guardian of the Great Seer, the Buddha's treasury of Dhamma was Venerable Ānanda. He had a wide knowledge of Dhamma, like an eye for the whole world. He dispels the darkness of the world.

1054. Possessing various knowledges, mindfulness, and deep wisdom, Arahant Ānanda, a great seer, is holding Dhamma jewels like a mine of gems.

1055. The Buddha's instruction has been respectfully followed by me. The Buddha's path has been fully followed by me. I lowered the heavy load of defilements. I rooted out the fetters of existence.

These verses were said by Arahant Ānanda.

Section of Forty Verses

The Verses of Arahant Mahā Kassapa

1056. A monk should not socialize with big crowds. If a monk lives in the midst of these crowds, chances are that his mind will be distracted. He will have a hard time developing one-pointedness of mind. Living a life attending to other people's duties is painful. A monk should understand this danger. Therefore a monk should avoid socializing with big crowds.

1057. The sage does not visit the families of supporters. If a monk wonders among families, chances are that his mind will be distracted. He will have a hard time developing one-pointedness of mind. He will be greedy for the delicious food the people offer and will desire more. He will miss the goal that brings true happiness to his life.

1058. Noble people consider that the respect and homage that comes to them is like a pile of mud. Desire for honour is like a fine dart that is hard to pull out. Inferior people never give up gains and honours.

1059. One day, coming down from the forest, I entered the city and was going on my alms round. I saw a leper eating. With a compassionate mind and for his wellbeing, I approached him.

1060. That leper offered a lump of rice into my bowl with his rotting hand. As he was placing the rice into my bowl, one of his fingers broke off and accidently fell in.

1061. After accepting that meal, I sat beside a wall and ate. Neither while I was eating, nor once I had eaten, did disgust arise in my mind at all.

1062. If a monk is contented with whatever food is offered on his alms round, his own urine as medicine, living under a tree as shelter, and wearing a rag robe, indeed such a monk will live at ease anywhere in all the four directions.

1063. Some people almost faint trying to climb up the mountain where I live. The heir of the Buddha, the monk Kassapa is now very old. But with full mindfulness, clear awareness, and supported by his psychic powers, he climbs up the mountain.

1064. Returning from his alms round, the monk Kassapa climbs up that rocky mountain. He is freed from fear and terror. He meditates without clinging.

1065. Returning from his alms round, the monk Kassapa climbs up that rocky mountain. Among the people who are burning with defilements, he quenched himself. There he meditates without clinging.

1066. Returning from his alms round, the monk Kassapa climbs up that rocky mountain. He is freed from all taints. He has done what had to be done to end suffering. He meditates without clinging.

1067. That region spread with Kareri trees is very delightful. The trumpeting of the king elephants makes this region even more beautiful. These rocky mountains delight my heart.

1068. There, the streams have beautiful pure water. Their cool water is the colour of blue clouds. In this night, the whole mountain is filled with the lights of fire flies. I really love this rocky mountain.

1069. With crags like huge clouds, like peaked roofed houses, with king elephants' trumpeting that beautifies the entire region, I really love this rocky mountain.

1070. Soaked with the rain all the time, that region is really beautiful. Those mountains called "Naga" are inhabited by Seers. The peacocks' cry resonates throughout the area. I really love this rocky mountain.

1071. Since I practice the Dhamma giving it top priority, maintain mindfulness well, and develop Jhānas, this rocky mountain is very suitable for me. As a monk who desires wellbeing and since I practice the Dhamma giving it top priority, this rocky mountain is very suitable for me.

1072. As I am a monk who lives in comfort and since I practice the Dhamma giving it top priority, this rocky mountain is very suitable for me. As I am a monk with an unshaken mind who desires to meditate, and since I practice the Dhamma giving it top priority, this rocky mountain is very suitable for me.

1073. The sky is the color of blue flax flowers, covered with flocks of various birds. I really love this rocky mountain.

1074. Lay people are not found anywhere in this area. But this area is home to herds of deer, and full of flocks of various birds. I really like this rocky mountain.

1075. The water in the streams here is fantastic. There is a wide flat surface on this huge rock. The mountain is populated by monkeys and deer. It is covered with oozing moss. I really like this rocky mountain.

1076. I have a one pointed mind. I penetrate everything with insight. That understanding of reality makes a wonderful joy arise in me. Even the fivefold music won't make me happy like this True Dhamma.

1077. A monk should not be busy with building projects in the monastery. He should avoid evil people. If a monk is not content with few wishes, he will become greedy and desirous of delicious food and drinks. Then he will miss the goal that brings true happiness to his life.

1078. A monk should not be busy with building projects in the monastery. A monk who desires his own wellbeing should avoid such things that make him tired, fatigued and pained. Truly, such things don't lead to calmness of the mind.

1079. The one who overestimates himself talks arrogantly. He does nothing but wander around with a stiff-neck thinking, "I am supreme."

1080. Truly not supreme, the fool thinks of himself as though supreme. Wise people do not praise such stiff-minded fools.

1081–82. "I am supreme, I am not supreme, I am worse, or we are equal." These ideas come from conceit. If one is not agitated with such conceit, that person who has an unshaken and a perfectly still mind, is wise, virtuous, and practices calming the mind. Such a person is praised by the wise.

1083. If a monk has no respect for his fellow monks, he will be as far from the true Dhamma as the earth is from the sky.

1084. But, if a monk always lives mindfully, with shame and fear of wrong doing, his holy life will come to growth. His repeated existence will come to an end.

1085. Even though a monk is wearing a robe made of rags, if he is conceited and vain, he doesn't have any beauty whatsoever. He is like a monkey wearing a lion's skin.

1086. If a monk is not conceited or vain, prudent, and keeps his faculties restrained, he truly deserves the rag robe, the flag of liberated ones. He is like a lion in a mountain cave.

1087. About ten thousand gods have gathered here. They are glorious and have psychic powers. They all have come from brahma worlds.

1088. They are standing worshiping with joined palms the General of the Dhamma, Arahant Sāriputta, who has great energy, Jhānas, and a still mind.

1089. Homage to you, thoroughbred of men, homage to you, best of men. We can't even find out the object you meditate on.

1090. The knowledge field of the Buddhas is extremely wonderful. It is very profound. Even though we are really skilled in penetrating very subtle fields, like skillful hair-splitting archers, we can't understand the Buddha's knowledge field.

1091. When Arahant Kappina saw Arahant Sāriputta who was being worshiped by the group of gods, a smile arose on Arahant Kappina's face.

1092. Throughout the entire excellent knowledge field of the Buddha, except for him, I am the outstanding person in the practice of austerity. There is no one equal to me. In the austerity practice, I became the foremost monk.

1093. The Buddha's instruction has been respectfully followed by me. The Buddha's path has been fully followed by me. I lowered the heavy load of defilements. I rooted out the fetters of existence.

1094. This monk Kassapa has immeasurable qualities. He does not cling to robes, shelters, or food. He is like a beautiful lotus flower grown in the water that has bloomed from unsoiled water, spreading a sweet fragrance. He is entirely liberated from all existences.

1095. That great sage has a neck called mindfulness, hands called faith, and a head called wisdom. That great wise sage always lives with a quenched mind.

These verses were said by Arahant Mahā Kassapa.

Section of Fifty Verses

The Verses of Arahant Tāḷapuṭa

1096. I am here really thinking, when indeed shall I go into a thick forest filled with beautiful waterfalls and live there alone with a mind free from craving. When indeed shall I contemplate with insight all existences as impermanent? When indeed shall I fulfill these wishes?

1097. Like a sage wearing a torn robe, when shall I wear a robe? When shall I live with a mind free of self-identity and craving? Having removed passion, hatred and delusion from this mind, when shall I live peacefully in a forest?

1098. This is an impermanent body, suffering from various diseases, like a nest disturbed by ageing and death. So, having penetrated this body with insight, and rid of fear, when shall I live alone in a forest?

1099. Craving is the producer of fear, bringer of pain, twining around this entire life. So, having taken a sharp sword made of wisdom, when shall I cut the creeper of craving into pieces? When indeed shall I fulfill these wishes?

1100. There is a lion-throne called serene and insight meditations. There are swords of enlightened ones made of wisdom, of fiery might. So, having seated on that lion's throne, holding those swords, when shall I aggressively fight against the army of Māra? When indeed shall I fulfill these wishes?

1101. I really like the association of superior people. They respect the Dhamma, have realized the nature of reality, have unshaken minds, and have conquered their senses. When shall I associate with such superior people? When shall I practice the Dhamma very hard with them?

1102. I really want to achieve Nibbāna. Undisturbed by laziness, hunger, thirst, winds, heat, insects, and snakes, when shall I live in a mountain cave? When indeed shall I fulfill this wish?

1103. The Great Seer, the Supreme Buddha, realized these Four Noble Truths. So, with a still mind, developed wisdom and mindfulness, when shall I realize these Four Noble Truths that are very hard to realize? When indeed shall I fulfill this wish?

1104. I really like to develop Jhāna. So, by wisdom, based on that one-pointedness of mind, when shall I see these innumerable sights, sounds, smells, tastes, touches and thoughts as though they were a blazing fire? When indeed shall I fulfill this wish?

1105. When shall I live without worrying about people talking harshly to me? When shall I live without being overjoyed when people praise me? When indeed shall I fulfill these wishes?

1106. When shall I understand with wisdom these Five Aggregates of Clinging, both internally and externally, as no more than just wood, grass and creepers? When indeed shall I fulfill this wish?

1107. Getting soaked by the rain, when shall I walk on the path walked by the enlightened ones in the forest in the rainy season? When indeed shall I fulfill this wish?

1108. In the thick forest, among mountains, the peacocks cry out. When shall I wake up to that cry and meditate, wishing for Nibbāna. When indeed shall I fulfill this wish?

1109. There are great rivers such as the Ganges, Yamunā, and Sarasvatī. There are fearful slopes. There are huge lakes. Without touching them with my feet, when shall I cross over these things using my psychic power? When indeed shall I fulfill this wish?

1110. Like a king elephant separated from the herd, when shall I meditate separated from the desire for all the objects that appear to be attractive connected with sensual pleasures? When indeed shall I fulfill this wish?

1111. When shall I live happily realizing the teaching of the Greatest Seer, the Buddha, like a poor man stricken by debt and, after being repeatedly oppressed by rich men, has found a golden treasure? When indeed shall I fulfill this wish?

1112. Hey mind! Didn't you beg me repeatedly for years to give up the home life? How much did you beg me to become a monk? Now I have become a monk. Hey mind! Why don't you meditate now?

1113. Hey mind! Didn't you beg me to go to a forest and meditate sitting on a flat rock in the midst of mountains where birds cry and waterfalls flow? You told me that you really loved it, didn't you?

1114. Hey mind! It is because of your request that I became a monk giving up all my possessions and valuables, relatives, friends, enjoyments and all sorts of sensual pleasures. Now I have entered the forest. But now why don't you make me happy pushing me on the path to Nibbāna?

1115. Hey mind! This mind doesn't belong to others. It is mine. Now I am ready for the battle against defilements. But why are you crying now? I have realized that everything is subject to destruction. That is why I renounced the household life desiring the death free-state, Nibbāna.

1116. Hey mind! Do you know what the great physician, the best of men, the supreme trainer of people, the speaker of good, the Supreme Buddha, said about this mind? "This mind is very fickle. It is like a monkey always moving in the forest. It is very hard to restrain this mind for one who is not rid of lust."

1117. Ordinary people are sunk in ignorance. They attach to these sensual pleasures that are attractive, sweet and delightful. They seek existence repeatedly and wish only for pain. Taking them away from the good, this mind puts them in hell.

1118. The great forest resonates with the cries of peacocks and herons. One is exposed to leopards and tigers. One will have to give up longing for life. Don't let this opportunity pass you by. Hey mind! Wasn't it you that urged me to become a monk?

1119. You asked me to develop meditation, develop spiritual faculties, develop spiritual powers, develop enlightenment factors, develop one-pointedness of mind and attain the Triple Knowledge in this Buddha's path. Hey mind! Wasn't it you that urged me to become a monk?

1120. You asked me to train in the way to the death free state, Nibbāna, and to develop the Noble Eightfold Path which leads to complete elimination of suffering, purification of defilements and leads to Nibbāna. Hey mind! Wasn't it you that urged me to become a monk?

1121. You asked me to contemplate the reality of the five aggregates of clinging, understand them as suffering and abandon the desire towards them that generate suffering, thus putting an end to suffering in this very life. Hey mind! Wasn't it you that urged me to become a monk?

1122. You asked me to contemplate these conditioned things as impermanent, painful, empty, selfless, misery, and as a burden, and to restrain the mind from the wandering defilements. Hey mind! Wasn't it you that urged me to become a monk?

1123. You asked me to become ugly with a shaven head! You asked me to take a bowl and join the begging monks as someone who was cursed by suffering in saṁsāra. You asked me to live in accordance with the instruction of the Greatest Seer, the greatest teacher. Hey mind! Wasn't it you that urged me to become a monk?

1124. You asked me to restrain the mind. You asked me not to get attached to families and sensual pleasures while going on the alms round. You asked me to live like the moon on a full moon night. Hey mind! Wasn't it you that urged me to become a monk?

1125. You asked me to live in a forest, survive on alms food, live in a cemetery, wear robes made of rags, meditate without sleeping and always desire to practice austerities. Hey mind! Wasn't it you that urged me to become a monk?

1126. Hey mind! Just like a person wishing for fruits who, having planted trees, wishes to cut down those trees, you push me into this impermanent unstable saṁsāra, don't you?

1127. Hey formless mind! You travel far and wander alone. But after this I won't follow your commands again! Sensual pleasures are really painful, bitter and very fearful. Certainly I wander, pointing my face only to the direction of Nibbāna.

1128. Hey mind! I didn't become a monk because of bad luck, nor from shamelessness towards begging for food, nor because of a fickle mind, nor because of banishment, nor because of not having any other livelihood. But, I have agreed that I won't go under your control ever again.

1129. Having few wishes is always praised by the Superior people. When disparagement is abandoned, suffering fades away. Hey mind! Wasn't it you that urged me to become a monk? Then why are you now trying to go back to your previous bad habits?

1130. Craving, ignorance, pleasant and unpleasant things, attractive forms, happy feelings, and pleasing sensual pleasures: all these have been vomited up by me. I don't need to swallow back what has already been vomited.

1131. Hey mind! Everywhere I went, I have followed your advice. Therefore, in many previous lives, I didn't make you angry. You were born from me, but you don't have any gratitude. That is why, for a long time, you dragged me through this painful journey of saṁsāra.

1132. Hey mind! Because of you one time I became a Brāhmin, another time I became a millionaire, another time I became a king, another time I became a trader, another time I became a servant, and another time I became a god.

1133. Because of you, I went to the asura world, because of you I went to hell, because of you I went to the animal world and because of you I went to the ghost world.

1134. Hey mind! You are trying to deceive me again and again. You try to show me illusionary, magical pictures time after time. You try to play with me as though a crazy man would. Hey mind! What have I done to you to deserve this pain?

1135. Hey mind! Formerly, you wandered where you liked, how you wished and how you pleased. But today, I will tame this disobedient mind with the hook of wise consideration, just as the hook holder tames a disobedient elephant.

1136. My great teacher showed me the reality of this world to be impermanent, unstable, and futile. Hey mind! Make me enter the path of the Great Victor, the Buddha. Help me cross the great flood of saṁsāra which is very hard to cross.

1137. Hey mind! Now the old mind is not here. Now you can't control me as you wish. I am a monk in the Great Seer's path. No one can harm those who are like me.

1138. Mountains, oceans, rivers, the earth, all conditioned things in the four directions, intermediate directions, and above and below are impermanent. All three planes of existence are disturbed by defilements. Hey mind! Which place are you going to be happy in?

1139. Hey mind! Now I am firm in strong effort. What can you do to me now? Hey mind! I am no longer under your control! Never will I touch the bag with an opening at each end filled with faeces. This human body is just like that, oozing filth from nine doors. Shame on this body!

1140. Hey mind! Wild boars and deer walk around in this beautiful forest with slopes and hills. The whole forest has been sprinkled with fresh water by the rain. Now you have entered a cave in this beautiful forest. Now be happy.

1141. The peacocks have beautiful blue necks, beautiful crests, beautiful tail fathers, and beautiful wings. When the sky thunders, those peacocks scream. Hey mind! Now you are meditating in this cave. Be happy about it.

1142. In the rainy season, the grass grows four inches high. The forest has blossomed with flowers like clouds. There on those mountains I lie on the ground. That grassy land is like a new bed for me. It is very soft.

1143. Yes, I tame you like a king commands a servant. Whatever has been obtained to maintain this life is enough for me. I am not lazy, therefore I will make you fit for Nibbāna like someone who transforms cat skin into a well worked bag.

1144. I tame you like a king commands a servant. Whatever has been obtained to maintain this life is enough for me. I will bring you under my control by my energy as a skilled hook holder tames a disobedient elephant.

1145. Hey mind! You have been tamed very well, like a superior elephant was tamed. Like someone who tames a horse, I also was able to travel on the blissful way to Nibbāna. That path to Nibbāna was only ever followed by the great beings who guarded their mind.

1146. Hey mind! I have bound you to the meditation object as one chains a king elephant to a post. Since I established mindfulness well, I was able to guard and control the mind. With that well developed mind, I escaped from all existences.

1147. When senses contact objects, it is through that contact that this mind follows the wrong path. I cut off that wrong path with wisdom. Using meditation, I put the mind back on the right path. You should see the arising and the cessation of the suffering in this saṁsāra. You should be liberated from suffering. In that way, be fortunate as the son, as an heir to the Buddha.

1148. Hey mind! I was deluded in such a way that I saw impure things as pure, impermanent things as permanent, unpleasant things as pleasant and selfless things as things with self. The mind misled me like a foolish boy. But now, you associate with that compassionate Great Sage who cut off all fetters.

1149. Hey mind! Like a deer roaming freely in this delightful mountain decorated in clouds, I live in this forest freely, undisturbed by anything. Hey mind! Undoubtedly, you have been defeated.

1150. Hey mind! If any men or women get caught up in your desire, go under your control, and delight in sensual pleasures, they all will sink into ignorance and go under Māra's control. All those who wish to be reborn again and again—they are all your followers.

These verses were said by Arahant Tāḷapuṭa.

Section of Sixty Verses

The Verses of Arahant Mahā Moggallāna

1151. We live in the thick forest surviving on alms food. We are content with whatever comes into our alms bowls, and we have inwardly perfectly still minds. We tear apart the army of Māra.

1152. We live in the thick forest surviving on alms food. We are content with whatever comes into our alms bowls, and we knock down the army of Māra as a king elephant knocks down a bamboo hut.

1153. Sitting at the foot of a tree, we always meditate. We are content with whatever comes into our alms bowls, and we have inwardly perfectly still minds. We tear apart the army of Māra.

1154. Sitting at the foot of a tree, we always meditate. We are content with whatever comes into our alms bowls, and we knock down the army of Māra as a king elephant knocks down a bamboo hut.

1155. Hey lady! You have a body like a hut made of a skeleton, sewn together with flesh and tendons, smelly, filled with filth. You think greedy thoughts of others' bodies. Shame on you!

1156. Hey lady! You are like a bag of filth, with a body covered up with skin, with lumps on your chest. You are like an ugly ghost! There are nine openings in your body flowing with filth all the time.

1157. Filth flows from nine openings in your body. Your body makes an evil smell. Your body is the biggest obstacle for one who is on the path to Nibbāna. A monk desiring this pure goal should definitely avoid that pit of filth.

1158. If any person knows, as I know about this body filled with filth, he would avoid women as one avoids a sewer on a rainy day.

1159. [Lady:] Great recluse, what you just said is extremely true, you are a great hero. But some men attach to my body like an old bull sinks in mud.

1160. [Arahant Moggollana:] If one would think of painting the sky yellow or any other colour, that will only tire him out.

1161. My mind is also like that sky. It is inwardly perfectly still. You foolish lady, don't try to attack me and meet with trouble, just as a moth perishes in presence of a huge flame.

1162. See the true nature of this body which is created by putting together tendons and bones. Foolish people delight in and appreciate this body. This body is subject to diseases and doesn't have a permanent stability.

1163. Still, one should see the true nature of this body even though it is decorated with jewels and ornaments. This skeleton wrapped up in skin is made attractive by its clothes.

1164. The feet are painted with colours and the mouth produces fragrances having chewed mint. These things are enough to trick a fool but do nothing for one who seeks Nibbāna.

1165. The hair is braided stylishly, and the eyes are painted with makeup. These things are enough to trick a fool but do nothing for one who seeks Nibbāna.

1166. This filthy body is kept as a nicely decorated pot. This is enough to trick a fool but does nothing for one who seeks Nibbāna.

1167. The deer hunter set out the traps, but the deer did not get caught. While the deer trapper was crying, having eaten the bait, we left quickly.

1168. The hunter's trap was smashed. The deer didn't get caught. While the deer trapper was crying, having eaten the bait, we left quickly.

1169. The earth shook when the great Arahant Sāriputta, possessed of many noble qualities, attained final extinguishing at passing away. Then there was terror and hair-raising excitement.

1170. Truly, conditioned things are impermanent. They are subject to arising and passing away. Having arisen, they cease. Tranquilization of this causality is happiness.

1171. One should see these Five Aggregates of Clinging as something that belongs to someone else, not oneself. Such wise people can understand this very subtle Dhamma as skilled archers split a hair with an arrow.

1172. One should see these conditioned things as something belonging to someone else, not oneself. Such wise people can understand this very subtle Dhamma as skilled archers split a hair using another hair.

1173. Just as someone tries to find help immediately after being hit by a sword and as someone immediately tries to put out a fire on his head, with strong mindfulness a monk should immediately try to abandoned sensual desire.

1174. Just as someone tries to find help immediately after being hit by a sword and as someone immediately tries to put out a fire on their head, with strong mindfulness a monk should immediately try to abandon desire for existence.

1175. Living with a well-developed mind, bearing his final body, my Great Teacher, the Buddha, instructed me to do that task. Following that instruction, I shook the Palace of Migāra's mother (Monastery) with my big toe.

1176. Liberating from defilements and achieving Nibbāna cannot be done with a slack effort or little effort.

1177. But this young monk is a supreme man. Having defeated the army of Māra, he bears his final body.

1178. Flashes of lightening fall upon the flat land between the mountains Vebhāra and Paṇḍava. There, in a mountain cave, that monk meditates. He is a son of the incomparable Buddha, the one with an unshaken mind.

1179. He is calm and well restrained. He lives in faraway forests. He is a sage. He is the heir of the Great Buddha. He is even worshiped by Brahma.

1180. Brāhmin, pay homage to the heir of the Buddha, the Arahant Kassapa who is calm, well restrained, and a sage who lives in faraway forests.

1181-82. Even if one is born as a Brāhmin among humans one hundred times in the clan of Brāhmins and studies Veda scriptures, if one worships such a Brāhmin who is well versed in the three Vedas and has reached the climax of his studying, that worshiping is not worth even a sixteenth part of the homage paid to the Arahant Kassapa.

1183. Every morning that monk attains the Eight Liberations forwards and backwards. After that he goes on his alms round.

1184. Brāhmin, don't trouble such a monk. Do not destroy yourself. Have confidence in the enlightened sage, the one with an unshaken mind. Quickly join your palms and pay homage. May your head not split open!

1185. He who is caught up with the journey in saṁsāra does not see the true Dhamma; he follows a crooked road, a wrong way.

1186. If a monk is infatuated with gain and honour and obsessed with conditioned things, he is like a worm smeared with excrement. He is going on a meaningless, empty journey.

1187. But see that Arahant Sāriputta coming. How pleasant he looks. He has developed both serene and insight meditations to their culmination and has become liberated from both ends called serenity and insight. He is inwardly perfectly still.

1188. See that Arahant Sāriputta coming. He doesn't have the darts of defilements and he has destroyed all fetters. He has attained the Triple Knowledge and defeated the army of Māra. Therefore he became the unsurpassed field of merit for humans, worthy of gifts.

1189. About ten thousand gods have gathered here. They are very glorious, and possessed of psychic powers. They all have come from the world of the brahma Purohita. With joined palms they are standing worshiping Arahant Mogallāna respectfully.

1190. Homage to you, thoroughbred of men! Homage to you, best of men! You are freed from taints. Great sage, truly you are worthy of the gifts of the world.

1191. Humans and gods respect that monk. He was born in this world of ageing and death. Finally, he was liberated from that world. Now he lives unsoiled by any formations, like a white lotus flower grown in the mud that has bloomed and stands tall.

1192. In an instant, that monk can know the thousand-fold world system. He is equal to Mahā Brahma, possessing supernormal powers. He possesses the knowledge of seeing the passing away and rebirth of beings. He also sees the gods at the appropriate time.

1193. Whatever monk has crossed over saṁsāra by wisdom, virtue and calmness, he is equal to Arahant Sāriputta. Arahant Sāriputta is indeed excellent in those three factors.

1194. In an instant, I can clone myself a hundred thousand times. I can use my psychic power as I wish. I have mastered my psychic powers.

1195. That monk is in the path of the Greatest Sage who attained perfection of one-pointedness of mind and perfection of true knowledge, and is liberated from craving. That wise monk from the Mogallāna clan, with a still mind, ripped out the defilements as a king elephant rips out a thin entangled vine from a tree.

1196. The Buddha's instruction has been respectfully followed by me. The Buddha's path has been fully followed by me. I lowered the heavy load of defilements. I rooted out the fetters of existence.

1197. I became a monk with the wish to achieve one goal. That, I have achieved. I have cut all fetters.

1198. Hey Māra! There was a Māra called Dussi. That Māra troubled Kakusaṇḍha Supreme Buddha and his chief disciple Vidhura. As a result, having being born in hell, this is how that Māra suffered there.

1199. Having troubled Kakusaṇḍha Buddha and the great disciple Vidhura, this is how that Dussi Māra suffered immensely falling into hell. That hell being is always struck with hundreds of iron spikes, all causing separate pain.

1200. The monk who knew that result of kamma is now a disciple of the Gotama Budhha. Hey Māra! Having troubled such a monk, are you going to fall into trouble?

1201. In the middle of the great ocean there are astonishing, heavenly mansions lasting for an eon. They are like shining gems. In those mansions, brilliant deities dance, radiant, of various colours.

1202. The monk who knows that is now a disciple of the Buddha. Hey Māra! Having troubled such a monk, are you going to fall into trouble?

1203. The Buddha instructed me to do a task. Following that instruction, I shook the Palace of Migāra's mother (Monastery) with my big toe while other monks were watching.

1204. The monk who knows that is now a disciple of the Buddha. Hey Māra! Having troubled such a monk, are you going to fall into trouble?

1205. Using psychic powers, with his big toe, he shook the Vejay-anta Palace of the God Sakka and made the gods tremble. I am the monk who did that task.

1206. The monk who knows that is now a disciple of the Buddha. Hey Māra! Having troubled such a monk, are you going to fall into trouble?

1207. That monk asked the God Sakka in the Vejayanta Palace thus: "Sir, do you know the way to be liberated from craving?" God Sakka answered explaining the Dhamma as he learned it. I am the monk who asked the question.

1208. The monk who knows that is now a disciple of the Buddha. Hey Māra! Having troubled such a monk, are you going to fall into trouble?

1209. There is a heavenly assembly called Sudhammā. The Great Brahma was present there. That monk asked the Great Brahma thus: "Sir, formerly you had a wrong view. Do you still have that wrong view? Look at the bright light of the Supreme Buddha who travels through the Brahma World surrounded by great disci-ples." I am the monk who asked that question.

1210. Then the Great Brahma answered that monk thus: "Vener-able Bhante, I no longer have that wrong view which I had for-merly.

1211. How could I say today that I am permanent or eternal? I see the bright light of the Supreme Buddha who travels through the Brahma World surrounded by great disciples."

1212. The monk who knows that is now a disciple of the Supreme Buddha. Hey Māra! Having troubled such a monk, are you going to fall into trouble?

1213. Using psychic powers, the peak of the great mountain Meru was touched by a monk and in the Indian Sub-continent, the country called Pubba Videha, that land where people sleep on the ground was touched by that monk. I am that monk.

1214. The monk who knows that is now a disciple of the Buddha. Hey Māra! Having troubled such a monk, are you going to fall into trouble?

1215. Truly, the fire does not think, "I shall burn this fool," but the fool is burnt having touched the burning fire himself.

1216. Hey Māra! In the same way you also try to trouble an enlightened monk. Like a fool who will burn his body having touched the burning fire himself, are you also going to get burnt?

1217. Hey Māra! In the past, Dussi Māra accumulated much demerit having troubled the Buddha. Do you think that your demerit will not haunt you?

1218. Hey Māra! Because of your evil deeds, you have heaped up demerit, resulting in pain for a long time. Hey Māra! Therefore, don't wish to commit evil having opposed the Supreme Buddha and monks!

1219. In this way, Arahant Moggallāna threatened Māra in the Bhesakala forest. Then Māra was disappointed and disappeared on the spot.

These verses were said by Arahant Mahā Moggallāna.

Section of Seventy Verses

The Verses of Arahant Vaṅgīsa

1220. Even when I have become a monk in the Buddha's path, having abandoned the home life, still these inferior, unwholesome thoughts chase after me.

1221. Even if a well-trained army of a thousand great archers with a thousand arrows surrounded and shot me, still I would not run away. I won't surrender.

1222. But even if more women than that were to come, they wouldn't be able to tempt me. I am well established in the Dhamma.

1223. I learned this path of Nibbāna from the Buddha, who was born in the clan of the sun. My mind is always firm in that path.

1224. Hey Māra! While I am treading that path, you come to trouble me. But see what I will do to you. Without giving any opportunity for you to see my way, I will one day die.

1225. If someone abandons the dislike of meditation, abandons the liking of sensual thoughts, abandons inferior thoughts and doesn't generate craving at all, he is liberated from craving. He who is freed from craving is called a monk.

1226. In the sky, on the earth and in this entire world, whatever is made of the four great elements is impermanent and is decaying. Liberated ones have realized that truth.

1227. But people with defilements are deluded by forms, sounds, smells, tastes and tangibles. If someone lives without defilements, devoid of desire for those things and unattached to them, he is called the sage.

1228. Ordinary people have got caught up in the wrong teachings. Having been entangled in sixty-eight wrong views, they argue. But without getting entangled in any of those wrong views, and entirely freed from them, if one doesn't talk about unnecessary things, one is called a monk.

1229. This wise monk has had a still mind for a long time, not deceitful, prudent, rid of craving and attained to the Supreme peace of Nibbāna. This sage awaits his time to attain final extinguishing at passing away.

1230. Gotama, abandon conceit and the path to conceit completely. If you are infatuated with the path to conceit, you will regret it for a long time.

1231. Saying bad things about others covers up their good qualities. Conceit strikes people down. By these things, people fall into hell and grieve there for a long time.

1232. Having followed the path of Nibbāna and practiced a proper training, the monk who attained victory never grieves. He experiences fame and happiness. Wise people call him the one who sees the Dhamma having attained to the truth.

1233. Therefore, eradicate the spikes of defilements. Practice energetically. Abandon the hindrances. Attain to purity. Abandon all conceit. Achieve the calmness of the mind. Achieve true knowledge and put an end to this suffering.

1234. Oh, Gotama (speaking to Ānanda Bhante), my mind is burnt with desire for sensual pleasures. My mind is on fire all around. Oh, with compassion teach me a way to extinguish this fire of lust.

1235. [Ānanda Bhante:] Certainly, you have been deluded by distorted perception. That is why your mind is on fire. Immediately abandon the sign of attractiveness which arouses lust.

1236. Understand all formations as things belonging to others, as pain, and not as self. Immediately extinguish the great fire of lust. May you not burn in the fire of lust again!

1237. With a unified and a perfectly still mind, develop the meditation on unattractiveness. Establish mindfulness on the contemplation of the body. Live with a mind disenchanted with the world.

1238. Develop the insight meditation which is devoid of signs of defilements. Cast out the conceit deeply rooted in the mind. By the full understanding of conceit, live calmly.

1239. [Vaṅgīsa Bhante:] Indeed one should speak such words that don't harm oneself and others. Such words are truly called well spoken words.

1240. One should speak only pleasant words. Everyone welcomes such words. Avoiding evil words, one should speak agreeable words.

1241. Absolutely, truth is the immortal word. Truth is the eternal law. Therefore, superior people are firm in truth, meaning, and Dhamma when they speak.

1242. Whatever word that demolishes fear, leads up to Nibbāna, and puts an end to suffering, was spoken by the Buddha. That is the best of all words in the world.

1243. Arahant Sāriputta's wisdom is very deep. It is amazingly profound. He is very skilled in teaching how to distinguish between the right and wrong path. Arahant Sāriputta teaches the Dhamma to monks using that great wisdom.

1244. He can preach the Dhamma in brief and at length. He can preach elaborately. His voice is sweet like the sound of the myna bird. When he is preaching, his profundity becomes more and more evident.

1245. Everyone hears his sweet and lovely words. Monks like to listen to those delightful words that are very pleasant to hear. Monks give ear with joyful and happy minds.

1246. Today is a full moon. Five hundred liberated monks have assembled together to perform the pure recitation of virtues. These monks have destroyed the fetters of existence and rebirth and have been liberated from suffering. All these monks are Great Seers.

1247–48. Just as a wheel-turning universal king surrounded by his ministers goes all around this earth bounded by the oceans, even so, the unsurpassed Supreme Teacher wanders surrounded by his disciples, possessed of the Triple Knowledge, who have won the battle defeating the army of Māra.

1249–50. All these liberated monks are sons of the Blessed One. There is no weakness in them at all. The destroyer of the dart of craving, the Buddha, who was born to the clan of the sun, is surrounded by more than a thousand of these monks. The Buddha taught us about the undefiled Nibbāna where there is no fear from any direction.

1251. The monks listen to the pure Dhamma taught by the fully enlightened Buddha. In the midst of the community of monks, the sight of the Supreme Buddha is extremely astonishing.

1252. The Buddha is the seventh Seer among Great Seers. The Blessed One is called "Nāga." The Buddha makes the rain of Dhamma fall upon the disciples, just like a heavy rain storm.

1253. Getting up from the daytime resting place, I have come here desiring to see the Great Teacher. Great hero, your sacred feet are being worshiped by your disciple Vaṅgīsa.

1254. Look at the Great Teacher. The Buddha closed Māra's devious path entirely, broke up the spikes of defilements, and now wanders freely. The Buddha teaches the Dhamma analytically and releases these beings from all bonds and defilements.

1255. The Buddha taught this path of Nibbāna solely to cross the flood of defilements. When that path was explained in various ways, monks were firmly established in the unstirred Nibbāna.

1256. The Dhamma realized by the Buddha overcomes everything and brings the light of Dhamma. The Blessed One taught that Supreme Dhamma to the group of five monks for the first time.

1257. When such a well taught Dhamma is available, and knowing it, why wouldn't someone take the practice seriously? Therefore, always pay homage to the Blessed One and practice the path of the Buddha diligently.

1258. With strong energy, in the generation of Buddhas, the Arahant Koṇḍañña always lives experiencing the happiness of seclusion.

1259. Whatever fruit is to be obtained by a disciple following the Great Teacher's instruction respectfully, that fruit was obtained by all the diligent disciples.

1260. Arahant Koṇḍañña is mighty. He attained the Triple Knowledge. He is skilled in reading others' minds. He is the heir of the Buddha. Arahant Koṇḍañña worships the sacred feet of his Great Teacher.

1261. Those disciples with Triple Knowledge live having left Māra behind. When the Buddha, who crossed over suffering, stays upon the flat surface of the Isigili rocky mountain, the Great Teacher is surrounded by the disciples.

1262. Arahant Moggallāna's psychic power is incredible. He has a taint-free, liberated mind. Arahant Moggallāna can read the minds of monks with his mind.

1263. In this way, these liberated ones possess many various skills. The Gotama Buddha, who is possessed of all good virtues, is surrounded by such skilled monks.

1264. The shining moon in the cloudless sky is delightful. The spotless sun also shines brilliantly. The Great Sage, Aṅgīrasa, is exactly the same. You outshine the whole world by your fame.

1265. Formerly, I was a skilled poet. I was intoxicated by my skill. I used to wander from village to village and from city to city. One day, I saw the fully enlightened Buddha who had crossed over everything.

1266. The Great Sage, the Buddha, who crossed over all suffering, taught me the Dhamma. My mind was so pleased with that Dhamma. Indeed, it is for our wellbeing that we were gifted with this Triple Gem.

1267. I learned the words of the Buddha very well. I studied the aggregates, the elements, and the sense bases. I became a monk in the Buddha's path.

1268. Many men and women follow the Buddha's path. Truly, Tathāgatas appear in the world for the wellbeing of many.

1269. The monks and nuns entered the path of Nibbāna and attained Nibbāna. Truly, the Buddha attained enlightenment for our wellbeing.

1270. The Buddha, the one with eyes of Dhamma, who was born in the clan of the sun, taught these Four Noble Truths out of compassion for all beings.

1271. Suffering is a Noble Truth. The arising of suffering is a Noble Truth. The overcoming of suffering is a Noble Truth. The Noble Eightfold Path leading to the extinguishing of suffering is also a Noble Truth.

1272. Thus, these Four Noble Truths have been taught in this Dhamma. I also have seen them just as they are. I have obtained the ultimate goal. The Buddha's path has been fully followed by me.

1273. My entering into the Buddha's path is truly a blessing. It was in the presence of the Buddha that I learned this well expounded Dhamma. I too realized that Great Dhamma.

1274. I have obtained the perfection of profound knowledges. I have purified my divine ear. I have achieved the Triple Knowledge. I developed psychic powers. I am skilled in reading others' minds.

1275. You are my Great Teacher who has perfect wisdom, who cuts off all uncertainties and doubt in this life. I ask you respectfully about my preceptor. That monk's virtues were well known; he had an extinguished mind; he passed away at the Aggālava Monastery.

1276. His name is Nigrodhakappa. It was the Blessed One who gave that name to that noble monk. That monk always followed the path putting forth energy. Seeing the profound Dhamma, longing for Supreme Nibbāna, that monk lived worshiping the Buddha.

1277. Great Sage of the Sākyans, the sage who sees everything, we all wish to know about that monk. Our ears are ready to hear. You are indeed our Great Teacher, our unsurpassed Great Sage.

1278. The Sage who sees everything, you are sitting in the midst of monks like the god Sakka, surrounded by gods. Sage of great wisdom, tell us about that monk and dispel our doubt. Did that monk attain final extinguishing at passing away?

1279. Ignorance is what makes the whole world deluded. Those ties of defilements, bases of doubts that go along with ignorance, none of them are found in the Tathāgata. Indeed, you are called the Supreme Eye of all beings.

1280. The Buddha dispersed all defilements as the blowing wind disperses a mass of rainy clouds. If the Buddha hadn't done that, the whole world would have been enveloped in darkness, and people who shine in wisdom would never be found in the world.

1281. Wise sages are the great beings who illuminate this world. My great hero, the Buddha, I think that you are such a being. We have come to the Greatest Sage who sees reality and who knows reality. Oh Blessed One, sitting in the midst of monks, reveal the Nigirodhakappa Bhante's life to us.

1282. True meaning is released from that sweet voice. Words are sent forth in a beautiful way. Teach us the Dhamma in a sweet tone, tell us with beautiful words in a sweet tone, like a goose stretching out its neck. We all will listen with upright hearts.

1283. The Buddha eliminated the round of birth and death completely and achieved purification by cleansing all evil. I shall make the Buddha speak about the sweet Dhamma. The Buddhas don't act according to mind's desires as ordinary people do. The Buddhas always act with wise consideration.

1284. The Buddha teaches the Dhamma in a very clear way. The Buddha has perfect wisdom. We accept all the virtues of the Buddha. Worshiping with joined palms, we tell you, "Oh the Great Teacher of great wisdom, please, give us knowledge."

1285. Great hero, with perfect wisdom, Great Sage with perfect realization, release us from delusion! We too like to listen to the Dhamma as one longs for water when burned by heat in the summer. Make the rain of Dhamma fall on us!

1286. Surely our Nigrodhakappa Bhante lived the holy monk-life expecting the ultimate noble goal. Did he achieve the goal? Did he attain final extinguishing at passing away? Or did he die with defilements? We wish to know about that.

1287. [The Blessed One:] In this world formed by mentality and materiality, for a long time his mind was stuck in the rapid flood of Māra. He cut off craving for the whole world. He passed beyond the round of birth and death forever (so spoke the Blessed One, the one with the best types of knowledge.)

1288. [Vaṅgīsa Bhante:] Supreme Seer, hearing your voice I am pleased. Whatever I asked from the Blessed One was never in vain. The True Brāhmin never deceived me.

1289. That monk is also a disciple of the Buddha who acted as he spoke. Using wisdom, he cut the deceitful net of Māra.

1290. The Blessed One discovered everything about Nigrodhakappa Bhante. Kappa Bhante has truly crossed over the realm of Māra, which is very hard to cross.

1291. Best of humans, best of gods, I pay homage to you, the Great Buddha. I also pay homage to the great elephant, the great hero, Arahant Nigrodhakappa, who was born from your heart; he is truly your son.

These verses were said by Arahant Vaṅgīsa.

Index

Numbers refer to verse numbers for each Arahant.

Mahamegha English Publications

Sutta Translations
Stories of Sakka, Lord of Gods: Sakka Saṁyutta
Stories of Brahmas: Brahma Saṁyutta
Stories of Heavenly Mansions: Vimānavatthu
Stories of Ghosts: Petavatthu
The Voice Of Enlightened Monks: The Theragāthā

Dhamma Books
The Wise Shall Realize

Children's Picture Books
The Life of the Buddha for Children
Chaththa Manawaka
Sumina the Novice Monk
Stingy Kosiya of Town Sakkara
Kisagothami
Kali the She-Devil
Ayuwaddana Kumaraya
Sumana the Florist
Sirigutta and Garahadinna
The Banker Anāthapiṇḍika

For more information visit www.mahamevnawa.ca

Mahamegha Publishers - Polgahawela

Tel : 037 2053300, 0773 216685 **e-mail :** mahameghapublishers@gmail.com

Thripitaka Sadaham Poth Madura - Borella

Tel : 0114 255 987, 077 4747161 **e-mail :** thripitakasadahambooks@gmail.com

Made in the USA
Middletown, DE
07 October 2020